MAKING MUSICIANS

Making Musicians

A PERSONAL HISTORY OF THE BRITTEN–PEARS SCHOOL

Moira Bennett

BITTERN PRESS

First published 2012
The Bittern Press
6 Mundays Lane, Orford,
Woodbridge, Suffolk, IP12 2LX

Phototypeset by Agnesi Text, Hadleigh, Suffolk
Printed and bound in Great Britain by EAM Printers, Ipswich, Suffolk

A catalogue record for this book is available from the British Library.

ISBN 978–0–9571672–0–9

To my son Julian,

and in memory of my three older children,

David, Nickie and Bill

The Bittern Press gratefully acknowledges the generosity of the following Benefactors and Donors, without whom the publication of *Making Musicians* would not have been possible:

Benefactors

Arup
Kenneth Baird
Peter Bowring
Lady Cave
John Evans
David Heckels
John McLaren
Colin Matthews
Louise and Reicke Schweitzer
Derek Sugden
Françoise Sutton
Rita Thomson

Donors

Humphrey Burton
Virginia Caldwell-McNay
Paul Cassidy
Pat Cooke-Yarborough
Pamela Embleton
Hugo Herbert-Jones
William Jacob
Corinne Laurie
Lady Maddocks
John Owen
Christopher and Christine Tinker
Dame Gillian Wagner
Jenni Wake-Walker

Contents

Acknowledgements

My first thanks must go to John Owen at whose suggestion and encouragement this book was started and without whose help none of it would have been possible. I would also like to thank the Britten–Pears Foundation, particularly Dr Colin Matthews, who listened sympathetically to my proposal, and the Trustees who agreed to finance all the travel expenses incurred during the initial research. I am grateful, too, for the assistance I received from the staff at the Britten–Pears Library during the early stages of the project.

I owe a tremendous debt of gratitude to my colleagues at the Bittern Press, without whose untiring efforts we would never have succeeded in bringing the book to publication: Kenneth Baird, who undertook to oversee all the fund-raising required; Jill Burrows, whose work and advice as editor and designer have been invaluable and Philip Reed, whose experience and expert knowledge have been a source of strength.

I wish to thank all the benefactors and donors whose kindness and generosity have been very humbling; without their support we could not have proceeded and I want them to know how enormously grateful I am to all of them.

I want to thank all the musicians and other contributors who so generously responded to my request for interviews and who contributed their unique memories of the time they spent at the School. In particular I must thank Graham Johnson who kindly read the text in its very early form, whose advice and memories were incredibly useful, and above all for his agreeing to write the Foreword.

I would also like to thank Nigel Luckhurst who made an extremely generous arrangement making his extensive photographic archive available to us, and to Arno Drucker, Jean Uppman and Arup who very kindly gave us permission to use their photographs. I am indebted to Peter Clifford and Michael Richards of Boydell & Brewer for undertaking the marketing and distribution of the book.

Without any one of these the book could never have reached publication and I hope that they all know how grateful I am.

M.B.

Foreword

A great deal about Benjamin Britten has been written since his death, but far less about Peter Pears, whose achievements, like those of even the greatest performers, will inevitably be overtaken by his successors (or so they may allow themselves to believe). He was the composer's lifelong 'mouthpiece', as he once described himself, but for today's musical public his unique position at Britten's side, though surely safe in historical terms, is gradually fading. Britten remains alive and well, for composers are immortal in a way singers can never be.

It is not Moira Bennett's concern to discuss here whether anyone could, or ever will, sing Britten's music remotely as well as Peter Pears. Instead her book salutes the great singer's imagination and vision as a teacher and as the founding father of a school that has gone from strength to strength. It was Pears, still in his thirties, who had been a moving force in the founding of the Aldeburgh Festival, and many of its innovations can be laid at his door. The School, with Britten's strong support in the early stages, was the last of these great ideas. In the years following the composer's death the singer, bereaved but unbowed, was determined to carry on. If there were to be no more new compositions, the green shoots of renewal would be seen (and heard) in the form of young singers and instrumentalists. These pupils would be nurtured with the greatest teaching whilst drinking in the calm and peace of this ravishing corner of Suffolk.

As a young pianist immensely privileged to accompany masterclasses given by Pears and others, I understood, even then, that something of historical importance was happening. This was a project that was unique in this country – then, as now, touched with the magic of everything that Aldeburgh was, and is, as a centre of music. Peter's determined energies, and his altriuism (decades before it was obligatory, for concert halls and festivals in search of funding to tick boxes concerning education or outreach) swept everything before him; he engaged (in both senses) distinguished teachers and musicians of every kind, and they are all affectionately discussed here.

Moira Bennett was not a musician by training (although her knowledge of music was soon extensive) but she was at the centre of everything, too young at the time to be the 'mother of the School', but occupying something of that role. She made it a happy place. Moira enchanted and delighted Peter and had a similar effect on me and countless students. It is perhaps unfair that someone so clever and amusing and sympathetic should also have been so good at her job. That she has decided to write down what she remembers of those times is a boon for all of those who perhaps need reminding that Aldeburgh and its Festival, even in those days, did a great deal more good for music in the bigger picture than the promotion of a single great composer's work.

Graham Johnson

Introduction: The Setting

The Britten–Pears School for Advanced Musical Studies in its original form and in its later incarnation as the Britten–Pears Young Artist Programme represents an important and lasting memorial to its founders, the composer, conductor and pianist Benjamin Britten and the tenor Peter Pears. It has fulfilled magnificently their vision for specialized music education in the United Kingdom. From small, tentative beginnings the School achieved an international reputation for excellence and contributed substantially to the successful careers of hundreds of talented young musicians from all over the world. Many of those now at the very top of their profession received encouragement and training at an early stage in their professional careers from Britten, Pears and their like-minded colleagues.

The Suffolk landscape in which the activities of both the Aldeburgh Festival and the Britten–Pears School are located is fundamental to an understanding of Britten and his music. Britten and Pears made their home on the exposed Suffolk coast, in Aldeburgh, some thirty miles south of Britten's Lowestoft birthplace. It provided them with the sympathetic environment essential for their creativity. It was here, in 1948, that, with Eric Crozier, the writer, director and librettist, they established the Aldeburgh Festival. Concerts, recitals, talks and exhibitions were initially mounted in the churches and halls of the town itself as well as in churches in neighbouring towns and villages such as Orford and Blythburgh, and then, from the late 1960s, in the Concert Hall lovingly converted

An event in the first Aldeburgh Festival: E. M. Forster gives a lecture on George Crabbe in the Baptist Chapel. Britten sits alongside him.

© Kurt Hutton

A rough sea off Aldeburgh beach, 1949

> *If wind and water could write music, it would sound like Ben's.*
> YEHUDI MENUHIN

from the Victorian shell of an old maltings at Snape, a village a few miles inland from Aldeburgh.

Although the School was eventually situated at Snape, alongside the Maltings Concert Hall, the ancient town of Aldeburgh has always been central to the life of the School. Poised between the sea and the River Alde, it is benign in the summer, but bleak and desolate in the winter, when the only sounds seem to belong to the sea and the wind and the screeching gulls.

'Aldeburgh' literally means 'old fort' and at one time it was a great ship-building centre; two of Sir Francis Drake's ships were built here. However, when the river began to silt up, ship-building ceased and the town became reliant on fishing. Throughout its long history Aldeburgh has been constantly battered by the wind and the sea, which, with its ever-changing moods, dominates the town. The Moot Hall, these days virtually on the beach, used once to be in the centre of the town and all the churches and houses that once lay to its east are now drowned beneath the waves.

Anyone who has lived in Aldeburgh will have come to understand the power of the sea and will be familiar with the sound of the maroon in the middle of the night, soon followed by the thudding of heavy boots as the volunteer lifeboatmen run through the silent streets down to the beach to man the lifeboat and do their utmost to rescue those out in the wild North Sea whose lives might be in jeopardy. It is this atmosphere, where one is all too aware of the complete dominance of the sea, that is so perfectly reflected in Britten's *Peter Grimes*. It is certainly the experience of all those who live here and those from all over the world who have come to perform and to study here.

Although Aldeburgh is now very much seen as a holiday destination, with throngs of people visiting in the summer, milling up and down the long High Street, coming here to enjoy the music or the sailing or the beach or the golf or its unique August Carnival, it also has a dark history of fear and menace, dating from a time when the townspeople were caught between the ubiquitous smugglers and the forces of law and order embodied by the coastguards; each could be as dangerous and violent as the other.

People learned the hard way the wisdom of trusting no one and keeping their own counsel; under the surface the echoes of that dark and threatening time are still present and the descendants of those early inhabitants look long and hard at newcomers before accepting them.

Fishermen still haul their boats up the beach and sell their catch fresh from the sea, but they are far fewer than in the days when fishing was the main occupation in the town. It was this atmosphere, formed by the North Sea and its coast, that Britten loved and that led him to establish his home with Peter Pears in Aldeburgh, first on the seafront and later on the northern edge of the town, at the Red House.

Since the establishment of the Aldeburgh Festival in 1948 the Suffolk landscape that Britten found so inspiring has

Aldeburgh High Street in a bygone age

> *Suffolk, the birthplace and inspiration of Constable and Gainsborough, the loveliest of English painters; the home of Crabbe, that most English of poets; Suffolk with its rolling, intimate countryside, its heavenly churches big and small; its marshes with those wild seabirds, its grand ports and its little fishing villages. I am firmly rooted in this glorious county.*
>
> BENJAMIN BRITTEN
>
> on being made a Freeman of the Borough of Lowestoft

Snape Maltings Concert Hall, 1967

It was the Englishness *of the place that hit me so hard, and to study Britten's music in those surroundings, his surroundings, was an amazing privilege.*

Henry Ingram

become known to music-lovers throughout the world, but for many of the students making their first visit to the School, particularly those from the United States and Canada, it was unfamiliar and the environment was a revelation.

Snape lies four miles inland from Aldeburgh, above the River Alde, overlooking the typical flat Suffolk landscape of marshes, reeds, water and wide skies with its magical, ever-changing light. Although a relatively small village today, in its time Snape was a much more important place than Aldeburgh. It was settled by the Romans two thousand years ago and was an important burial place for Anglo-Saxon rulers. It is thought that many inhabitants of Snape perished in the plague and as a consequence the village dwellings were subsequently built closer to the river. The Church, once at the centre of the village, is now some distance from the houses, shops and pubs.

In the eighteenth and nineteenth centuries Snape was well known for horse racing and one important race meeting that always drew considerable crowds was held every year through a century and a half.

For many years the heart of the village was the maltings, a large complex of industrial buildings, providing the malt for the brewing industry and employment for the villagers. The main building, with its iconic roof, was transformed into the Concert Hall in 1966–67, with the building alongside becoming the Britten–Pears School in 1979.

Newson Garrett started building the maltings at Snape in the middle of the nineteenth century. He was a ship-owner, grain transporter, Lloyds agent and a Mayor of Aldeburgh. One of his daughters, Elizabeth Garrett Anderson, was the first woman doctor in Britain and the first woman Mayor of Aldeburgh, elected in 1908. Another daughter was Dame Millicent Garrett Fawcett, an early feminist and pioneer in education.

The buildings are in traditional mid-nineteenth-century industrial style using red brick from the local Snape brickworks and with timber floors and deep timber roofs constructed with local shipwright skill. The malthouse roofs were once finished with Welsh and Italian slates, and the turning bays and low buildings with red clay pantiles. When roof slates and tiles were replaced, the roofs were covered with asbestos slates or sheeting which was well suited to the industrial scale of the buildings.

At a later period the maltings was owned by Swonnells & Sons, who also owned the maltings at Oulton Broad, near Lowestoft, but by 1965 they were obliged to sell all the buildings at Snape, including twenty houses and the pub, making all those employed redundant and bringing great hardship to the village. The maltings was on the market for six months and was eventually bought by a syndicate of local businessmen including George Gooderham, a Suffolk farmer. Over time, by selling the houses, individually priced between £1000 and £1500, Gooderham managed to raise the necessary funds to acquire the entire complex.

In the early years of the Aldeburgh Festival many of the performances were staged in the Jubilee Hall in the centre of the town: it was in this small hall that two of Britten's stage

Tom Savage, a maltster at Snape, *c.* 1890

Industrial buildings on the maltings site at Snape awaiting renovation

works, *The Little Sweep* and *A Midsummer Night's Dream*, received their first performances. As the Festival grew and developed into an international success, the management of the Festival, led by Britten and Pears, sought a larger venue more suitable for opera and for the growing audience. The opportunity arose to negotiate a long lease on the maltings at Snape – now part of George Gooderham's portfolio of properties. The decision was taken to investigate the possibility of converting the main building into a modern concert hall and opera house.

In October 1965 Stephen Reiss, the Aldeburgh Festival Secretary and Manager, wrote to the civil engineer Ove Arup asking whether Arup Associates would survey the disused maltings and offer an opinion on the potential of the site. The survey was completed later that year and Arup was asked to prepare designs and supervise a contract for the Concert Hall to be ready in time for the 1967 Festival. The Queen opened the hall on 2 June 1967.

Two years later, to the horror of musicians and audiences way beyond Suffolk, on 7 June, the first night of the 1969 Festival, the Concert Hall was completely destroyed by fire. The cause has never been definitively established, but is thought to have been an electrical fault. Despite this devastating event, the rebuilding of the hall was immediately commissioned and, astonishingly, the work was completed within forty-two weeks, in time for the opening of the 1970 Festival. When the rebuilding was commissioned, further plans were prepared for carrying out improvements to vehicle parking, dressing-room accommodation and stage access within the turning bays alongside the main auditorium.

The only buildings that had been converted and that were covered by the lease were the maltings itself, which consisted of the main building, the germinating bay and the granary store. Over the ensuing years all the surrounding buildings began to fall into a state of disrepair with the paint morosely peeling off the woodwork and the access roads becoming increasingly pot-holed and unkind to the suspension of the audience's cars.

The great and the good arriving for performances given by internationally renowned artists would be greeted by hand-written parking directions and be directed between tatty and dilapidated buildings by one of George Gooderham's employees diverted from his usual responsibilities, a scruffily dressed and frequently rather irritable man. Few concert-goers realized that all this was not the responsibility of the Festival management and often expressed their dismay at the condition of the site. The roads, the parking spaces, the buildings and the employees were all part of George Gooderham's fiefdom. It was a take-it-or-leave-it situation; Gooderham was certainly was not going to be persuaded by any glamorous, international musicians to undertake costly repairs and renovations.

For many years efforts were made to purchase the freehold of the entire complex from George Gooderham but he always refused these overtures. He was a good, kind and loyal friend to many of those employed by the Festival and to a select few of the Aldeburgh Festival Council members, but his suspicions of 'the men in suits' ran deep, especially if they came from London.

After long years of negotiations and failed attempts to buy the maltings, ownership of the site passed to George's son Jonathan, who eventually reached an agreement for Aldeburgh Music to take responsibility for the buildings it occupies under the terms of a 999-year lease. While some parts of the complex remain near derelict, the Gooderham family – responsible for the shops and residential buildings – and Aldeburgh Music currently work alongside each other developing and improving the site. The area devoted to music has now been wonderfully renovated and converted into additional rehearsal and performance spaces.

It was the granary store adjoining the Concert Hall that was so successfully converted into the School in 1979, but the history and the vision for the School goes back much further than that. This is the story of its earliest beginnings, its subsequent achievements and the influence it has had on the music profession throughout the world, far outstripping even the most ambitious dreams of its founders.

The Beginnings: 1953–79

'One day we'll have a school here,' Benjamin Britten said in 1953 to Imogen Holst, the daughter of Gustav Holst and a great personal friend; she quoted the remark in an article in the *Musical Times* in 1977. Britten was speaking only five years after the establishment of the Aldeburgh Festival but from the early 1950s onwards Britten and Pears, the founders of the Britten–Pears School for Advanced Musical Studies, began to discuss their vision for a school with their friends and colleagues. They were both very aware of the need for specialized coaching for young musicians of outstanding ability at the start of their professional careers and they were conscious, too, that in Britain there was often a difficult gap in the crucial years between study at a conservatory and a musical career.

This desire to meet a need for gifted young musicians might have been uppermost in their minds, but it was not the only motivation behind the aspiration to establish a school. Britten was concerned for Pears's professional future and, later, Pears wanted to share the talents of his singing teacher, Lucie Manén, with as many young singers as possible. Gradually, and in consultation with their colleagues, their ideas began to take shape and the first masterclasses, which were held in 1972, showed the way forward for the future Britten–Pears School for Advanced Musical Studies.

Basil Coleman, a distinguished opera and television director and a long-standing friend and colleague of Britten and Pears, was present during some of those very early discussions about the School. He went on to have a close involvement with the School and to play a vital part in the future opera courses. He spent the decade between 1954 and 1964 in Canada and on his return to England directed a televised version of *Billy Budd*. He suggested to the BBC that there should be a production of *Peter Grimes*, recorded in the same way, a suggestion that was received enthusiastically, but changes at the Corporation took place and when the time came both Britten and John Culshaw, for the BBC, thought that the Maltings Concert Hall could serve as a television studio. Basil Coleman disagreed vehemently and withdrew from the project. This led to an estrangement with Britten lasting several years but following a reconciliation the two men again became trusted friends and colleagues.

Coleman, a gracious and elegant man with an unforgettable and beautiful speaking voice, is now in his nineties. Sadly, his sight is impaired but he continues to live alone in the London house that has been his home for over thirty years and that was to become a valued haven for a number of students of the Britten–Pears School to whom Coleman is still a beloved friend and mentor.

Talking about the School at the end of 2008, he said, 'One can't overestimate the importance of the actual building and its surroundings – they provided a perfect environment for the study of music.' When asked what he thought was behind the original vision for the School he said, unhesitatingly, 'Ben said to me that he wanted a school for Peter. The School was to be Ben's gift for Peter.' This touching story of Britten's concern for the tenor's future, beyond his professional singing career, when he might pass on his knowledge, perception and experience as a teacher, gives a further dimension to Britten's determination to establish a school. The writer, academic and publisher Donald Mitchell, another long-standing friend of Britten and Pears, made the same point when interviewed by Christopher Headington in 1990 during research for a biography of Peter Pears.

'Is it possible', Headington asked Mitchell, 'that in the last years of his life Peter was less interested in the Festival, or more interested in the School, at the expense of the Festival?'

Mitchell replied, ' Well, maybe. I think . . . that it would not have been an either/or situation, but he certainly became [. . .] greatly interested in the School . . . All that had been part of Ben's planning for the future, really, because he [. . .] was very wise about Peter, obviously, and saw that there would come a stage when Peter could no longer go on as a performer. He assumed that he, of course, would still be going strong as a composer and that the idea certainly was to have the School there for Peter . . . to let him fulfil – and continue to fulfil – his life and pass on his extraordinary experience as a teacher.'

Christopher Headington commented, 'It occurs to me and I'm sure that other people have made the same observation that although it is the Britten–Pears School – and rightly, of course – the School was really almost entirely Peter . . .' Mitchell replied, 'Oh, it was definitely built around Peter.'

This was certainly Basil Coleman's recollection of the very early beginnings and his ideas resonated with others when they were asked about those early days. Marion Thorpe, who was a very close friend of both Britten and Pears and for many years a Trustee of the Britten–Pears Foundation (now a Trustee Emeritus), agrees that this was an element in the early thinking about the School. She points out that Britten and Pears and some of their colleagues, notably Imogen Holst, shared a much broader vision of the future of music in this country in which advanced education would play a major part.

At the time, there were three institutions that had a profound influence on the thinking of Britten and Pears and with which they were both familiar. They had heard much about what was being achieved in Canada at the Banff Centre and also at Tanglewood in the United States. The pattern at Tanglewood, with its festival and summer school, most closely resembles the final structure of the School at Snape. The Boston Symphony Orchestra, under Serge Koussevitzky, had made Tanglewood its summer home in 1936 and the Tanglewood Festival dates from that time.

In 1940 the Tanglewood Music Centre was established as a venue for the intense training of gifted young musicians in their pre-profession years. While there they would be offered masterclasses, workshops and performance opportunities. Dating from the time that they were resident in the USA, Britten and Pears would have been aware of the activities at Tanglewood and the approach that had evolved there. (The Koussevitzky Foundation commissioned Britten's opera *Peter Grimes* and his *Spring Symphony.*)

And, of course, in England there was Dartington. In 1952 Imogen Holst came to live and work in Aldeburgh, assisting with the Festival and becoming Britten's music assistant. When Britten and Pears were first considering their vision for the future of the School they drew heavily on Holst's experiences at Dartington, where she had been the distinguished Director of Music and where she had been involved from 1942 to 1950. Pears described her work there as '*brilliant* – revealing, exciting'.

As Christopher Grogan recounts in *Imogen Holst: A Life in Music*: 'Back in the summer of 1953 Britten had mooted the idea of establishing a school of music in Aldeburgh and had told Imogen Holst that she should be its first Principal. Apart from the visit that year of a small group of students, who rehearsed choral music and a Mozart piano quartet with Britten and Imogen Holst, however, this idea had lain dormant in Britten's mind until the conversion of the Maltings in 1967. That done, Britten started to lay further plans for the extension of artistic activities on the site, including the fulfilment of his vision for a school. The idea was fully supported by Pears who, unlike Britten, was himself a keen teacher, and by Imogen Holst, for whom teaching and performing always represented two sides of the same coin.'

Rosamund Strode, who succeeded Holst as Britten's music assistant, was also a close friend and associate of Imogen Holst; she said that Holst was an enormous influence on the thinking and planning for the School, playing a major role in all the early discussions. Pears had himself taught at Dartington and

© Nigel Luckhurst

Peter Pears performing with Osian Ellis at Snape Maltings Concert Hall during the 1976 Aldeburgh Festival

his ideas for the School were very much the result of what he had observed there and were in tune with Imogen Holst's unique experience. The plans for a centre in Britain for advanced music education of the very highest standard gradually began to emerge.

However, by 1972, when the first masterclasses took place, there seems to have been another and more immediate motive behind the establishment of the School. During the 1950s Peter Pears had been suffering from vocal problems of one sort and another and in the 1960s the baritone Thomas Hemsley introduced him to a singing teacher, Lucie Manén, who was to play a crucial role in his professional career. Like many singers, Pears had anxieties about his voice and like many singers he continued to study with a teacher: Dawson Freer in the 1930s; Clytie Mundy in the 1940s, taking a refresher course with her in 1948 during a concert tour in the States; Eva de Reusz in the 1950s and Julius Gutmann in the early 1960s.

Then he was introduced to the brilliant German teacher Lucie Manén. There is absolutely no doubt that she did help him enormously; it was said at the time that she effectively took his voice apart and built it up again. She herself was later to say, 'I gave Peter back his voice.'

Both Britten and the great Russian cellist Mstislav Rostropovich had realized the extraordinary innate potential as a teacher Pears would be in a position to explore, once his singing career had come to its natural end. In 1965 Mstislav Rostropovich, with his characteristic love of jokes and his irrepressible enthusiasm, produced a 'contract' written in English, Armenian and Russian, in which Peter promised to establish a school. Pears put his name to it.

This was the year that Britten wrote *The Poet's Echo* for Galina Vishnevskaya. Britten and Pears were taking a sabbatical from their hectic concert schedule, and spent a holiday with the Rostropoviches in Armenia, where there might well have been further talk of future possibilities for Pears.

Even if there had been a few concerns about vocal problems, in both 1965 and 1966 Pears received rave reviews for recitals. On 4 January 1965 Colin Mason, reviewing the sixtieth-birthday concert for Michael Tippett, wrote in the *Daily Telegraph*, 'No English singer today matches Pears in the phrasing of words or of melody, let alone in the fusion of the two. He was in excellent voice and sang the dance cadenza here more articulately and effortlessly than on the gramophone record of ten years ago.' On 6 June 1965 Peter Stadlen, also in the *Daily Telegraph*, described the premiere by Pears of Lutosławski's *Paroles tissées* as 'gloriously sung'. In retrospect we know that his singing career was very definitely not over – his extraordinary triumph in *Death in Venice* was yet to come. Pears's gratitude and admiration for all that Manén did for him at a time when his future as a singer was uncertain was profound.

In 1974 Pears persuaded Faber Music to publish a book by Manén, *The Art of Singing*, for which he wrote a generous and enthusiastic foreword, even making a recording with Elizabeth Harwood and Thomas Hemsley that was included with the book. In the Foreword he writes, 'I have had the pleasure and privilege of working with her for a number of years. A lesson with Lucie Manén can indeed explore many tracts of unfamiliar country – anatomical, acoustic, aesthetic, scientific – but it is, finally, the acuteness of her ear which delights and astounds her pupils. An acute ear allied to prodigious knowledge is her chief weapon; and this Manual is the fruit of many years of concentrated listening as well as of singing and teaching. There is hardly a page without an original and revealing idea on it . . . I hail this Manual with gratitude and delight.'

The pianist Graham Johnson believes that Peter Pears felt that in Manén he had found the Holy Grail of singing teachers and that with typical generosity of spirit he wanted to share her undoubted gifts and her remarkable talent for teaching with as many singers as possible. Pears hoped to provide her with a platform where she would be fully appreciated.

After all the years of talking and dreaming about a school, there was the added impetus of the teachings of Lucie Manén. When the first weekend course and masterclasses for singers were held in September 1972 in, appropriately, what had been the germinating bay of the maltings, before the building had been transformed into the Concert Hall, it was her teaching methods that were to be given prominence. (This space was eventually to become the School's Recital Room.)

That autumn Graham Johnson was a twenty-one-year-old student at the Royal Academy of Music and it is a great tribute to his extraordinary talent that he was invited to be the

© Nigel Luckhurst

Peter Pears in the Recital Room at the Britten–Pears School during an English Song masterclass in 1979

Neil Mackie

accompanist for these very first classes. Among the singers taking part were Pamela Brady, Mary Clarkson, Glyn Davenport, Robert Gibbs, Mark Lufton, Neil Mackie, Anthony Ransome, Anthony Rolfe Johnson and Helen Sava. The composers whose works were studied were Britten, Purcell and Schubert.

The tenor Neil Mackie, then a young student from Scotland, had received the brochure for the weekend and a letter from Peter Pears which read, 'Are you interested in the enclosed? Students will not be charged for the events, but will be expected to find their own accommodation, and to contribute to their meals at Snape. I am also making it a condition of the singers being there for all the events. Can you let me know v. soon if you want to come and which Masterclass you prefer to be in? What about *Dichterliebe* in German and Scots? Who is the translation by? I can't remember.'

Neil Mackie became a distinguished singer and much admired teacher, Head of Vocal Studies at the Royal College of Music and later a Professor at the Royal Academy of Music.

Graham Johnson recalls that for those first masterclasses a makeshift stage had been built in the germinating bay, with paintings by Sidney Nolan from Britten's and Pears's collection hanging at the back of the room and seating arranged for a large number of people. Anne Surfling and Pamela Wheeler, who later became archive assistants at the Britten–Pears Library, where their encyclopaedic knowledge has proved invaluable to scholars and researchers, were present for that weekend – the first of many such visits.

*I had the good fortune to meet Peter Pears during my undergraduate studies at the Royal Scottish Academy of Music in Glasgow. Following a masterclass there (on Thursday, 25 April 1968), Peter persuaded me to give up the idea of school teaching, come to London, study at postgraduate level and then pursue a career in singing. 'Would you care to take part in an informal study weekend which I am organizing at Aldeburgh with Lucie Manén?' wrote Pears in a surprise letter to me in 1972. A tongue-in-cheek PP went on to suggest that I prepared '*Dichterliebe *in German and Scots'.*

However, the repertoire turned out to be Britten and Schubert – no surprise! The weekend began with a memorable Pears–Britten recital of English songs. I sang 'Before Life and After' [from Winter Words*] and Schubert's 'Nacht und Träume'. Graham Johnson was our excellent accompanist. Leslie Minchin gave a talk on singing Schubert in English translation while Peter spoke about English songs with special reference to Purcell and Britten.*

This stimulating weekend was the foundation of the Britten–Pears School as well as the start of a much valued friendship. As a result of the study weekend Pears became my vocal mentor and I began regular lessons soon after. I sent PP a cheque for the first ten lessons. The Master's reply: 'I have sent your cheque (finally!) to my bank. But I want you to know that I shan't expect another for a v. long time – if at all. Leave that to me and if I need it, I will ask for it.'

I enjoyed the privilege of inspirational lessons for almost fifteen years. Some days Peter would be too exhausted to give a lesson and so instead we would visit a nearby art gallery or share a meal together.

In many ways I bypassed the actual Britten–Pears School itself, although over the years Peter openly discussed its development with me.

Many of today's finest singers and accompanists are alumni of the Britten–Pears School. I am proud to have been a very small part of it and particularly to have been there at its birth.

NEIL MACKIE

The weekend began on Friday, 22 September 1972 with a public concert in the Maltings – sold out for the occasion of a Pears–Britten recital which included the composer's song-cycle Winter Words. *Among other papers and handbills on a table in the foyer were forms inviting observers to be present at the lectures and classes which were to follow during the weekend. The whole course was therefore open to observation for anyone in that audience. Many who were to become loyal supporters of the School accepted the invitation and found themselves attending lectures and classes with Pears.*

ANNE SURFLING AND PAMELA WHEELER

The audience for the first masterclasses was very distinguished and included Nancy Evans (later to become Pears's co-Director of Singing Studies), Eric Crozier and Murray Perahia, who had recently won the Leeds Piano Competition and was brought to Aldeburgh by Marion Thorpe. Although it was held in a converted, simple room, with the presence of so many celebrated musicians, it became a 'grand and glittery occasion' and was, as Graham Johnson says, 'terrifying for a twenty-one-year-old'.

He tells a touching story of Britten's thoughtfulness and understanding of youthful nerves. Anthony Rolfe Johnson was due to sing *Winter Words* and Graham Johnson, who was to accompany him, was very much aware that Britten, who had performed the cycle with Pears the night before, was sitting in the audience. The pianist was understandably nervous but, before he started to play, he looked around and to his immense relief saw that Britten was no longer there. Afterwards Britten came up to him and congratulated him warmly on his playing. 'But you weren't there,' said Graham Johnson. 'Well, I knew that you would be nervous and so I went and stood behind a screen while you were playing.'

Sue Phipps, Pears's niece and his and Britten's agent, was in charge of all the arrangements. During this period, Diana Hiddleston (the daughter of William Servaes, the General Manager of the Aldeburgh Festival) was assisting with the Aldeburgh Festival administration and was present for the whole weekend. She describes the atmosphere as 'electric'. The teachers and lecturers included John Carol Case, Lucie Manén,

Leslie Minchin, Peter Pears and Dennis Fry, Professor of Phonetics at University College, London. Apart from the actual masterclasses there were also workshops and discussions on such subjects as the language of lieder. Manén showed slides demonstrating her work on the physical and scientific aspects of the voice and Dennis Fry extended this by a lecture that included slides and tape recordings of the workings of the larynx. On the Saturday evening Pears – with occasional contributions from his colleagues – compèred a very informal gramophone recital. As one observer remembered, 'It was like a party to include us all and to invite us to share in this project.'

Olive Baldwin and Thelma Wilson, who were present for the weekend, had been attending the Aldeburgh Festival since 1964. Their chief academic interest was vocal music and they had been researching seventeenth- and eighteenth-century singers, particularly those for whom Purcell wrote music, had published articles in the *Musical Times* and *Music & Letters*, and would later contribute to the *New Grove Dictionary of Music and Musicians*.

Following this first weekend of classes at Snape, Graham Johnson received this letter from Peter Pears:

My dear Graham,

I want to thank you very much indeed for all the hard work you put into preparing and playing for the weekend. That it was a huge success was fairly clear, I think. It certainly achieved one of my mainest objects, which was to bring Lucie into full

Even allowing for inflation, the weekend was a bargain. The fee of £7.50 covered a Pears–Britten recital at Snape, two days of masterclasses and lectures, two lunches and a supper – 'but not including accommodation' the brochure stated.

We entered from the courtyard and we remember first seeing a young man with wonderful, bright red hair, who was, of course, Graham Johnson, the accompanist throughout. It soon became clear that we were going to hear a lot more of him. At the end of one session . . . we overheard Britten saying, 'Well done, Graham.' It was pleasing to find three good tenors, Neil Mackie, Anthony Rolfe Johnson and Robert Gibbs, who had a pleasant, light tenor voice and came to courses in later years but then decided not to pursue a professional career.

OLIVE BALDWIN AND THELMA WILSON

Graham Johnson

view (what a star she is at her job!) and to start something at Snape. I do hope that you will come and help again next year. I am putting July 27th – August 5th in my diary. Will you put it in yours?

Much love and again thanks,
Yours ever,
Peter

Lucie Manén, who played such an influential role at the start of the Britten–Pears School, was plainly a very unusual woman. A German singer of Jewish extraction, she had appeared at the Dresden Opera and, when her performing career faltered, had studied physiotherapy, which gave her a deep insight into the physical components of the voice. She survived the Second World War and the Holocaust and then came to Britain and married Otto John. He was a German who had played a role in the von Stauffenberg plot to assassinate Hitler and was a controversial figure, said to be involved in espionage in Germany when the country was split into East and West and perhaps in Britain before that. Manén had already had to overcome great difficulties and her personal life at the height of the Cold War could not have been easy.

She was quite obviously a remarkable singing teacher and, given her work as a physiotherapist, was able to demonstrate and share a unique understanding of the body and the voice. Pears offered her an opportunity that is given to very few. He was, in effect, offering her a school where she could develop her gifts as a teacher and reach young singers from all over the world. Sadly, due to later tensions and misunderstandings, she was unable to seize this chance and Pears's desire for her to be the linchpin of the new School was thwarted.

Graham Johnson remembers her as someone inclined to gossip and intrigue; he says that she was rather a foolish woman and that, although she had a deep understanding of resonance and the physiology of vocal production, she had far less interest in music itself, especially contemporary music. One night at a dinner party she told Britten that he didn't understand opera, which caused him to remark, rather ruefully, that that was somewhat unfortunate. Johnson remembers Britten, perhaps out of gratitude for all that she had done for Pears, treating her with 'infinite indulgence'. Johnson also says that she seemed not to understand the profound depth of the relationship between Britten and Pears and it is highly likely that this insensitivity was in part to blame for future disagreements. One of her colleagues, asked about her memories of Manén at the time, said, rather chillingly, 'Lucie Manén was not a kind-hearted woman.' Given the complexity of her personality, and the difficulties of her own life at the time, it is hardly surprising that a difficult situation arose in what was, inevitably, an intense atmosphere.

Despite their previously close friendship, Manén eventually quarrelled with Pears. She accused him of curtailing her career by expecting her to work only at Snape and of acting purely for reasons of his own monetary gain and out of personal greed. They disagreed over much, including plans for her to teach her methods to other singing teachers. If this were to happen, Pears wanted paying observers to be allowed to sit in on the sessions but she was convinced that this public exposure might prove to be humiliating for the teachers and she refused to agree. In any event, after bitter recrimination, Manén terminated her association with the School in 1975 and issued a public statement entitled, 'My Withdrawal from the Study Courses for Singers at Snape Maltings'.

This document is a long diatribe in which unpleasant accusations are made against Pears; she claimed that he wanted to exploit her, her work and her methods for his own selfish reasons. The statement ends, 'The incompatibility of P.P.'s and my approach to professional matters, to personal relationship – and that of his teacher – and his way of thanking me for my contribution to his career and "his" School of Singing makes it impossible for me to consider further co-operation with him.'

No one who knew Pears personally could ever have accused him of greed or of being obsessed by financial gain; in fact money for its own sake never seemed to interest him. This aspect of his character was well illustrated when in 1985 Sotheby's agreed to promote a charity auction to benefit the Aldeburgh Foundation. Donations of works of art and original manuscripts were sought from distinguished people who had been associated with the Aldeburgh Festival and their response was extraordinarily generous.

Pears had been collecting pictures all his life and, blessed with a very good eye, had over the years made some brilliant purchases. He possessed more pictures than could possibly be hung on the walls of the Red House and one would find valuable masterpieces stuffed into cupboards and pushed under beds. At the time, he possessed a small and beautiful cloud study which was thought to be by Constable but which had never been authenticated; he donated it to the auction with this instruction: 'If it is authenticated by the experts as being a Constable, you can have it for the sale. If it is not, I should like to have it back.' It was indeed authenticated by five experts and sold for £26,000, a very good price in 1985. This remarkably generous gesture was hardly the action of a greedy man and was entirely characteristic.

Equally characteristic was the fact that in 1979, despite all the acrimony, Pears invited Manén to join him on the jury of the Benson & Hedges Competition for Singers which was held annually at Snape. In those now almost unimaginable days tobacco companies were considered perfectly respectable, their money highly desirable and their contribution to the arts warmly acknowledged. Manén refused the invitation and wrote about her refusal, 'Peter P. asked me – in ever so sweet words – to come back to Snape and to join the Jury for the Benson & Hedges award – but I told him: Once I was his teacher, then his co-director but not his employee!'

However, many of her pupils remember Manén with lasting affection and respect and express gratitude for all that she taught them. The soprano Elizabeth Harwood, who died at a tragically young age, was always particularly close to Manén, sharing a long friendship with her and being always grateful for the benefit she was able to draw from her association with this unusual and talented teacher. It is plain that despite all the difficulties, Pears himself retained great fondness and regard for Manén, clearly shown in his correspondence with her after he suffered a disabling stroke in 1980, and it is interesting to speculate on what the future of the Britten–Pears School might have been had she not fallen out with him.

Following the success of the first masterclasses in 1972, it was agreed that the exercise, extended to a week in duration, should be repeated in 1973, and classes for singers were again held at Snape. Graham Johnson was joined by Roger Vignoles and the eighteen-year-old Simon Rattle to accompany the classes. Simon Rattle was, of course, to become a world-famous conductor: as Music Director of the City of Birmingham Symphony Orchestra he performed almost annually at the Aldeburgh Festival during the 1980s – for a while being a member of the Artistic Directorate for the Festival. He was knighted in 1994, and has been Chief Conductor of the Berliner Philharmoniker since 2002.

Johnson and Vignoles returned frequently for the singers' masterclasses and both worked extensively with Pears and with all those who taught at Snape. They were very important figures in the early development of the School – years that Graham Johnson describes as 'magical'.

Roger Vignoles had worked with the English Opera Group and was the répétiteur for Birtwistle's *Punch and Judy*, which was premiered in the 1968 Festival, conducted by David Atherton.

Vignoles was fascinated by differences in teaching methods and recalls a period that began and ended with two distinguished sopranos: Elisabeth Schwarzkopf and Galina Vishnevskaya. He says that Schwarzkopf used to stand well back from the student with her glasses on the end of her nose, exactly like a school teacher, and then analyse every detail of the work. He remembers her taking forty-five minutes over a song that was just one and a half minutes in duration. By contrast, Vishnevskaya was immediate and spontaneous; she would go right up to the student and work very closely with them, pressing their throats and touching their faces.

Vignoles recalls the additional elements during the courses: t'ai chi sessions offered by Gerda Geddes and Sue Phipps that did much to help singers with breathing, balance and posture as well as bringing a certain serenity to the often anxious and vulnerable students; as well as lectures related to the songs being studied: 'There were all the other add-ons at Snape. I remember particularly the amazing talks that Eric Crozier would give, one memorably on Verlaine and another on Thomas Hardy.'

Soprano Felicity Lott was to perform at Snape on many occasions. She recalls the masterclasses with Peter Pears and Joan Cross somewhat ruefully: 'I found it rather frightening at

1973
Courses for Singers

The Faculty included:
Joan Cross
Nancy Evans
Gerda Geddes (t'ai chi)
Thomas Hemsley
Imogen Holst
Lucie Manén
Peter Pears
Mary Thomas
Brian Trowell
Dr G. M. Ardran (throat specialist)

38 students attended, including
Mary Clarkson, Henry Herford, Felicity Lott
and singers from Denmark and Germany

We pianists were in a special position, between the students and the teachers, and this often meant not just coaching but pastoral care. There always seemed to be tears on Thursday! We were often required to supply amateur, armchair psychological advice for tearful singers.

Roger Vignoles

© Ben Ealovega

Roger Vignoles

> *The School had such an enormous influence on my career and I can remember every detail of the actual building. I always felt that Britten's spirit permeated every part of it and that that was what made it so special.*
>
> Roger Vignoles

the time and I have to admit that I arrived ill prepared which made it worse! But it was all such a wonderful experience.'

The soprano Joan Cross had worked with Britten and Pears in the English Opera Group and was the first Ellen Orford in *Peter Grimes* at Sadler's Wells, which she directed throughout the Second World War. She took leading roles in the first productions of other Britten operas – *The Rape of Lucretia*, *Albert Herring*, *Gloriana* and *The Turn of the Screw*. She gave masterclasses in the first years in the life of the Britten–Pears School and always retained a lively interest in all its activities, occasionally, in later years, attending masterclasses as an observer.

Prior to the summer courses for singers, in April a study weekend for pianists was held, conducted by the legendary Fanny Waterman, the co-founder with Marion Thorpe and Chairman of the Leeds International Pianoforte Competition. Sheila Moulds, who was a participant, remembers Fanny Waterman remarking that this was her first masterclass. Christopher Moulds, then aged five, also took part, playing duets with his mother. Among the students were Valerie Ashworth and Jonathan Dunsby, a regular pupil of Waterman, who gave a talk on her teaching. The pianist Benjamin Frith, too, was present for these masterclasses, which he remembers very well, along with a concert in the Maltings that included a performance of the Brahms D minor Violin Sonata performed by Paul De Keyser and Jonathan Dunsby.

Through 1972, 1973 and 1974 there was constant discussion about the future structure and the development of the School.

Among those taking part in these debates were Cecil Aronowitz, the distinguished viola player, a friend of both Britten and Pears; Donald Mitchell; Imogen Holst, and Steuart Bedford, who had been involved with performances at Aldeburgh since 1966 when he had been with the English Opera Group. He was invited by Colin Graham to come to Aldeburgh, where his family friendship with Britten – his mother, Lesley Duff, had sung in the first production at Glyndebourne of *The Rape of Lucretia* – developed into a close and long-lasting musical collaboration. Respected as a leading exponent of Britten's music, Bedford has enjoyed a substantial international conducting career in concert halls and opera houses. He conducted the world premiere of *Death in Venice*.

Bedford played a vital role in the development of the School, conducting many of the later School operas and many of the concerts given by the Snape Maltings Training Orchestra, which was formed by Cecil Aronowitz in 1974. The School was fortunate indeed to have the benefit of his unique experience and his deep insight into the Britten's music. The students not only admired and respected him but always enjoyed working with him and considered themselves extremely lucky to do so. In 1998 his connection with Aldeburgh was severed when he ceased to be an Artistic Director of the Festival. Although Bedford was formally assured at the time that the School would want him to continue to be involved, it was not until several years later that he returned to work at the School.

I owe it such a huge amount and I learned so much repertoire there. The time I spent at the School was always constructive and listening to the teachers going over and over details of a song gave the pianist the opportunity to experiment with his own work. Graham Johnson and I used to joke about the phrase 'half-pedal'. On one occasion Peter Pears, not quite happy with the sound, said, 'Could you do something a little different – maybe half-pedal?' and we supposed that perhaps it had come from a moment he must have had when working with Britten. We imagined him saying, 'What are you doing there, Ben?' 'Oh just a little half-pedal.'

ROGER VIGNOLES

The classes gave us a marvellous opportunity to learn about the techniques and problems of singers. Peter Pears's classes were always exciting, full of musical and vocal insights and he always showed courtesy to the students, each one of whom he tended to call 'my dear'. Looking back, it strikes us how much variety was built into the early courses, with lectures, mime, t'ai chi and even coach outings. The observers were seen as an integral part of the courses, some providing a chorus for end-of-course concerts and others producing props if there were staged opera scenes.

OLIVE BALDWIN AND THELMA WILSON

© Nigel Luckhurst

Nancy Evans, 1979

Cecil Aronowitz was asked to develop plans for string studies and Donald Mitchell to introduce academic courses. The Festival's General Manager William Servaes, a staunch supporter and later a generous benefactor of the School, was also deeply involved in the School's early development. At this time, 1974, a statement of intent was signed by Benjamin Britten, Peter Pears, Imogen Holst, The Countess of Cranbrook and Charles Gifford (office holders of the Festival's governing body), announcing the development of Snape Maltings as a Centre for Music Studies.

Peter Pears and Nancy Evans, who had sung in the English Opera Group and now worked as a vocal coach, were at the helm of song courses. Evans was later to be Pears's Co-Director of Singing Studies. They were in an unparalleled position to invite their friends to teach at the School and these friends, all part of a great musical family, were attracted to the concept and were happy to accept the invitation. For instance, Joan Cross, now living in Suffolk, prepared student singers for operatic roles between 1973 and 1976.

Nancy Evans continued for many years to coach, act as vocal consultant and to play a vital role in the careers of some of the finest young singers both in Britain and abroad. John McCormack, the celebrated Irish tenor, had once told her, 'Sure, Nancy, you're a cause for confession!' and none of her students will ever forget her remarkable beauty. Neither will anyone forget her essential sweetness of character and her gentleness – and her rather ribald sense of humour.

After an earlier marriage to Walter Legge, Evans had married Eric Crozier, the writer, director, and librettist of *Albert Herring*, *The Little Sweep* and, with E. M. Forster, *Billy Budd*. Crozier, too, played an important part in the School, giving lectures on the literary context of the works being studied during the song courses. He also directed the first School production of *The Rape of Lucretia* – the premiere of which he had directed at Glyndebourne in 1946.

Each year the courses became longer and more frequent. By 1976 a pattern was becoming established: there would be a course for singers around Easter with three or four more through the summer months.

The Britten–Pears Library, the collection of printed music, books, manuscripts, and paintings built up by Britten and Pears, which has over the years become a magnificent historic and archival resource for scholars and anyone interested in the creative and interpretative lives of its founders, first opened its doors to students and observers at courses at the School in 1976. A guided tour of the Library has continued to be a regular event for young performers coming to study at Aldeburgh and Snape.

The faculty for the fortnight-long course for singers in 1974 gives an indication of the status and experience of the teachers who were being attracted to Snape. Unfortunately Pears suffered a period of ill-health in 1974 and was ordered to rest. His scheduled classes were taken by John Carol Case, Thomas Hemsley and Donald Mitchell.

© Arno Drucker

Eric Crozier, Nancy Evans and vocal coach Ruth Drucker in 1994 during the English and American Song course.

© Nigel Luckhurst

Joan Cross during the 1976 Opera course, with Martin Penny at the piano

1974
Courses for Singers

The Faculty included:
Joan Cross Gordon Crosse Hugues Cuénod
Nancy Evans Pytt Geddes Thomas Hemsley
Lucie Manén Gerald Moore Peter Pears
Peter Purves John Shirley-Quirk Ian Spink

Accompanists
Graham Johnson Roger Vignoles

1975
Courses for Singers

The Faculty included:
Claude Chagrin Joan Cross Hugues Cuénod
Thomas Hemsley Hans Keller Lucie Manén
Peter Pears

The first masterclass given by Hugues Cuénod was the start of a remarkable teaching career at the School that was to last until the early 1990s. Students over the years were very lucky to be taught by this legendary tenor who was born in 1902 in Switzerland and who sang in all the great opera houses of Europe and the United States, finally making his debut at the Metropolitan Opera House in 1987, at the age of eighty-five. He had studied with Nadia Boulanger and had been invited by Stravinsky to sing the role of Sellem in the premiere of *The Rake's Progress*. He was a colleague and friend of Britten and Pears and would have been a natural choice to teach at these early masterclasses.

In 2008, aged a hundred and six, he talked with delight about his years at the School, remembering his students and, naturally, his colleagues the Belgian soprano Suzanne Danco and the Croatian soprano Jana Puleva Papandopulo who were later invited to join him as members of the faculty for French Song masterclasses. His students all remember his exquisite manners and charm and his gentleness as a teacher.

These high standards set in the early years characterized every aspect of the School. Many of the eminent practising musicians who taught there gave masterclasses nowhere else in the world. And from the start only the most gifted students were selected.

In 1975 there were two singers' courses in the summer; the first was 'Singing and Opera', followed by 'Lieder and Song'. Joan Cross directed students in scenes from *La Bohème* and

Rosamund Illing and James McDonald with Thomas Hemsley, 1977

© Nigel Luckhurst

Pauline Lowbury with Max Rostal, 1975

La traviata and Hans Keller contributed a lecture with the characteristically provocative title, 'What I expect and fear from a singer'.

Observers now began to be drawn into some of the sessions. Claude Chagrin, a mime and movement coach who had worked with the English Opera Group, ran stage-movement classes for students and observers combined, one of which was attended by Britten. Olive Quantrill, conductor of the Ipswich-based Olive Quantrill Singers and one of the trainers for the local amateur choir formed for the Festival each year, trained the ad hoc Observers' Choirs through the late 1970s and into the 1980s, achieving a remarkably high standard. The Observers' Choir made an appearance on stage in an excerpt from *The Magic Flute* at the end-of-course concert. These opera concerts were fully staged with scenery, props and costumes assembled from whatever came readily to hand.

By 1976 the summer programme had expanded to six courses. This was the year of the long hot summer and the Red House swimming pool was made available to any students and observers who wished to use it. There were three Singers' courses, a 'Baroque String Weekend' under the direction of Cecil Aronowitz, a two-day cello masterclass given by Mstislav Rostropovich and a twelve-day series of violin and viola masterclasses with Max Rostal.

The opera course focused on excerpts from Gluck's *Le cinesi* and the Christmas party scene from Britten's *Paul Bunyan*, supported by a chamber ensemble conducted by Michael

© Nigel Luckhurst

Mstislav Rostropovich directing a masterclass in the Jubilee Hall, 1976

© Nigel Luckhurst

Peter Pears, 1977

Lankester. Britten, by now seriously ill, attended the dress rehearsal in his wheelchair.

On 4 December 1976, after a long illness, Britten died. The impact was felt by everybody in the musical world but most deeply and intimately by everyone connected with the Festival and the School, who grieved for the man who had been the inspiration for all their activities. For Pears, whose personal loss was so great, the School seemed to provide some consolation and sense of purpose as, once more, he committed himself fully to the 1977 schedule of courses.

In 1974 Dr William Swinburne had been appointed Education Adviser. This was an important development. At the time Swinburne had recently resigned from his position as Director of Music at the North-East Essex Technical College but he retained an involvement with the institution as it became the Colchester Institute. Dr Swinburne's contribution to the development of the School has gone to some extent unrecognized. However, he does appear to have been something of a square peg in a round hole.

Jane Hawkesley, who was appointed as his assistant, believes that Swinburne's unceasing work played a much larger part in getting the School off the ground than is generally realized. She expresses admiration for his unflagging efforts. 'But', she says, 'he just didn't *get* Aldeburgh and although a distinguished figure in the world of music education, he seemed completely out of his depth. Apart from anything else, he was such a grumpy man with absolutely no charm or social skills.'

She recalls how on one occasion an influential musical journalist arranged to have lunch with Swinburne while in Aldeburgh. Hawkesley was present and describes an acutely embarrassing occasion as not only did Swinburne eat nothing, but actually read a newspaper throughout the meal. 'He was a remote man,' she says. 'Although I worked closely with him for five years, I felt that I did not know him at all.'

There are several instances on record where he wrote rather despairingly, 'I am not at all sure what my role is.' The clash of personalities and the resulting misunderstandings are, sadly, only too easy to imagine. He was deeply concerned with structure, administration and 'chains of command', illustrated by endless graphs and diagrams. He favoured a thoroughly bureaucratic approach, which is not surprising given his background, but very much at odds with the rather ad hoc way in which the School was actually growing. Reading his notes and reports of the time, one is struck by how far his vision of the future differed from the way that the School actually did develop.

He was convinced, and perhaps he was not alone in this, that the eventual aim should be for a full-time educational establishment, with an administrative director, in receipt of public funding. (It is impossible now to imagine the School operating with all the controls and interference that that would have entailed.) Swinburne certainly saw the future of the School as a completely independent body with its own director and its own administration, operating alone but in tandem

Council of Aldeburgh Festival–Snape Maltings Foundation

Sir Eugene Melville, Chairman

Sir Colin Anderson
Chairman of P&O

Mrs Frances Boothroyd

Peter Bowring
Chairman CT Bowring Ltd

Isador Caplan
solicitor and Trustee of the Britten–Pears Foundation

The Countess of Cranbrook

Peter du Sautoy
Chairman of Faber and Faber

Lord Goodman
Chairman of the Arts Council

HRH The Princess of Hesse and the Rhine   Imogen Holst

John Jacob
retired Naval officer

William Jacob
merchant banker and retired naval officer

Dr Donald Mitchell

Sir Claus Moser
banker, musician, statistician and academic

Peter Pears   Mrs Jeremy Thorpe

Sir David Willcocks
Director of the Royal College of Music

© Nigel Luckhurst

The Pichlar Quartet rehearsing in a dressing room at the Maltings during the First International Academy of String Quartets, 1977

with the Festival, which would, of course, in turn have its own general manager and administration.

One suspects that it was Swinburne's hand behind the rash of committees that were formed during this period. Chaired by Donald Mitchell, there was an Education Policy Committee, the members of which were Cecil Aronowitz, Peter du Sautoy (then Chairman of Faber and Faber), Imogen Holst, William Swinburne and Marion Thorpe. The Education Development Committee consisted of Cecil Aronowitz, Professor Peter Aston, Professor Boris Ford, Patrick Forbes, William Swinburne and William Tamblyn, Head of the Music Department at the Colchester Institute. These committees inevitably generated a vast amount of paper. Reading these documents one gets the impression that discussions about the future structure of the School went round and round while, in fact, the School was simply continuing to develop and grow in an unstructured and unique way, based on the experience of each year dictating the pattern of the next, and with the encouragement of musical excellence its sole guideline.

From 1972 until 1981 Sir Eugene Melville, former Ambassador and the Permanent British Representative to GATT (General Agreement on Tariffs and Trade), was the Chairman of the Council of the Aldeburgh Festival–Snape Maltings Foundation. Among its members were John and William Jacob, sons of General Sir Ian Jacob, who had been Assistant to Lord Ismay, the Military Secretary in Churchill's wartime cabinet, and who later became Director General of the BBC; and

Continued on page 48

© Nigel Luckhurst

Cecil Aronowitz and Imogen Holst during rehearsals for a concert given by the Snape Maltings Training Orchestra during the 1977 Aldeburgh Festival

Imogen Holst and Cecil Aronowitz prepared the Snape Maltings Training Orchestra for a performance in the 1977 Aldeburgh Festival, to be conducted by André Previn. In the event, Previn was indisposed and Holst and Aronowitz themselves conducted the concert, which was broadcast by the BBC. Imogen Holst recorded the following interval talk for Radio 3:

This concert that you are listening to was the first that the Snape Maltings Training Orchestra has given during an Aldeburgh Festival. Two years before this, Cecil Aronowitz had begun coaching a group of young string players, aged sixteen and upwards, at a weekend of rehearsals in the Maltings. On the Sunday afternoon they gave a performance to a very small audience; people hadn't turned up because they didn't know if the experiment was going to work. Those who did *come were astonished at the exciting sound. It was the real thing, and the listeners wondered how the players had managed it in such a short time. Well, it certainly helped that many of them already knew each other, and that a fair number of them were Cecil Aronowitz's own pupils. But there was more to it than that. For these young players weren't just good soloists in their own right; they were all chamber-music players, and they listened to each other.*

When that first experimental performance was over I went behind the stage to thank Cecil and told him what a joy it was to hear Mozart phrased like that. He said, 'It's only what I've been learning all these years from Ben.' And that's what the Snape Maltings Training Orchestra is about.

Since that first weekend the players have gone on from strength to strength, with large audiences and London concerts. Several critics have objected to the name that we've given to them. But it is *a 'training' orchestra; that's the whole point.*

As long ago as 1953, when I'd just begun working in Aldeburgh for Benjamin Britten, he said to me, 'What you and Peter and I have got to remember is that we're going to have a music school here one day.' That was long before the Maltings had been thought of. But Britten had meant what he said, and only a few months later he invited several students to his house on the sea-front and rehearsed the Mozart G minor Piano Quartet with them.

Britten was not a teacher; he said so himself. But throughout his working life, at every rehearsal he took, his players and singers learned from him. The music school that he'd hoped for came to birth at the Maltings in 1972 with a weekend for singers directed by Peter Pears. Britten was by then seriously ill, but during the next four years he was able to help us with his criticism and encouragement. Since his death, the Britten–Pears School of Advanced Musical Studies has become his memorial. We are building practice rooms in an unused wing of the Maltings, for until now the students have had to practise where ever they could fit themselves into an odd corner of the Concert

Hall; under the stairs, in the wardrobe-room, or in the passage where the scenery is brought in. Members of the Training Orchestra have put up with this discomfort because of the luxury of the super acoustic in our hall. If you are going to listen to the second half of this concert after the interval you will hear in my father's Brook Green Suite *a very quiet pizzicato passage; while we were rehearsing it I thought: 'Can we possibly risk playing as quietly as that? Will the people at the back of the hall be able to hear?' They did hear every note, for there is magic in the way the walls and the roof respond to the music that is offered to them.*

The Snape Maltings Training Orchestra is one of many things that are happening in the Britten–Pears School; there are string quartets, and madrigal groups, and rehearsals of Bach obbligato arias where the singers and players can learn from listening to each other. And I'm hoping that one day students will be taught conducting at the School, so that they can discover the need for a technique. And when they've got a technique, they may perhaps be able to convey what they have learned about rhythm from listening to Britten's recordings, where the music never sounds like one thing after another, but the rhythm and the form are always inseparable. This sense of 'wholeness' in the music is something that can't be expressed in words; it is what the players in our Training Orchestra are aiming at, and they get nearer to it in each performance.

IMOGEN HOLST

© Nigel Luckhurst

Snape Maltings Training Orchestra wind section, 1978

HRH The Princess of Hesse and the Rhine, a close personal friend of Britten and Pears, who did much to support their aims and ideals, including inaugurating the Hesse Student Scheme (which enabled cash-strapped students to attend concerts at the Festival in exchange for a little practical assistance) and the Festival's distinguished series of Hesse Lectures.

Melville frequently did not see eye to eye with Swinburne over the future of the School. The surviving documents from this period indicate that, despite the endless meetings, discussions and reports, it proved impossible to agree on the formation of a structure for the School. The disagreements arose between those – generally the musicians – who saw the School growing organically and the administrators and academics, such as William Swinburne and Donald Mitchell, who thought that more rigid structures were essential.

There was also a degree of tension between the Festival and the School. With hindsight it is obvious that the two organizations could work smoothly together only if one person were to oversee them both. However, that realization was not to emerge until much later.

It should be remembered that there were no models to copy; there had never been anything quite like the School in the UK and certainly not a school with such close and important links to an international festival. Everybody involved was feeling his or her way and reacting to the ideas and developments as they occurred.

American Friends of the Aldeburgh Festival

During these first years of the Britten–Pears School, its links with the United States and Canada assumed great significance and played an important role in its life and in its future.

Britten and Pears had very close and affectionate personal ties with friends in Canada and the United States, although their attitude towards US culture was rather ambivalent. In 1939 they had left the UK for North America, in the wake of their friends W. H. Auden and Christopher Isherwood. Initially they spent time in Canada, performing in Montreal, Toronto and Vancouver. Britten's *Young Apollo* – for piano, string quartet and string orchestra – was commissioned and broadcast by the Canadian Broadcasting Commission (CBC). They then settled in the USA, living in and around New York, where Britten's operetta *Paul Bunyan*, to a libretto by Auden, was first performed at Columbia University.

Three years later, after performing and travelling widely in the USA, they had come to feel their natural home was the UK, their homesickness spurred by reading an article about George Crabbe by E. M. Forster in the *Listener* while they were visiting California. After some delay waiting for a boat they were able to return in spring 1942.

As a result of this association with both the USA and Canada, and with so many friends and supporters in both countries, it is not surprising that they should have looked across the Atlantic when they first thought of creating groups overseas to generate support. The American Friends of the Aldeburgh Festival was established in New York in 1974.

While the Canadian Aldeburgh Foundation, which was set up in 1975, ran smoothly from its inception, and still functions efficiently and practically to this day, the American organization seems to have encountered difficulties all along the way and was finally disbanded some years ago. No trace of it remains and all efforts by the present administration of Aldeburgh Music to resurrect it have failed.

In its day the AFAF was an extremely powerful organization with a most distinguished Board of Honorary Directors and Members. Over time there were changes to the list of Honorary Directors with the appointment of the Hon. Kingman Brewster, Lord Inverforth, Olga Koussevitzky and Lady Penn. Similarly, there were changes to the Board of Directors. Mario di Bonaventura, Donald Gray, Rita Hughes, Caroline Lippincott, David Lloyd Jacob, W. Stuart Pope and Jane Gregory Rubin were members of the Board of the AFAF during its history. Caroline Lippincott and the conductor and composer Mario di Bonaventura were Presidents.

Mollie Webster, who served on the Board for many years, deserves special mention. She was a very active and enthusiastic Director and tremendously loyal to the Aldeburgh Festival, which she visited every year. She was herself born and bred on a farm in Framlingham, Suffolk. She married Daniel E. C. Webster, a descendant of the original compiler of *Webster's Dictionary*, and lived in New York. Her influence and her

American Friends of the Aldeburgh Festival

Alice Tully, Chairman
benefactor and patron of the arts, after whom
the Alice Tully Hall in the Lincoln Center NY is named

Francis Mason, President
museum director

Frank Taplin, Vice-President
benefactor and patron of the arts,
President of the Metropolitan Opera 1977–1984

Betty Randolph Bean, Executive Vice-President
Joseph Brinkley, Secretary
Thor E. Wood, Treasurer
Chief of the Performing Arts Centre, NY Public Library

Honorary Directors
Benjamin Britten OM CH
The Countess of Cranbrook
Sir Eugene Melville KCMG
Sir Peter Pears CBE
Claire Reiss
Mstislav Rostropovich
The American Ambassador to the United Kingdom
The British Ambassador to the United States
The UK Permanent Representative to the United Nations

American Friends of the Aldeburgh Festival

Directors

Betty Randolph Bean
Leonard Bernstein
Joseph Brinkley
Beekman Cannon
Aaron Copland
Ellis J. Freedman
Francis Mason jnr
Norman Singer
Clare Hawkes Stoff
Clementine Tangeman
Frank Taplin MBE
Alice Tully
Mollie E. C. Webster
James D. Wolfensohn
Thor E. Wood

personal knowledge of Aldeburgh were very helpful and she was in an ideal position to interpret one side to the other, a position that was particularly useful as there was to be a series of unfortunate misunderstandings.

The earliest mention of support for the Festival from the United States occurs in correspondence between Britten and Norman Singer in 1967 and the concept of a support organization in the United States might have been envisaged as early as that. Britten, Pears and Stephen Reiss (then General Manager of the Festival) visited the USA in autumn 1969 seeking financial support; Singer promoted recitals by Pears and Britten at Hunter College. However, the first formal acknowledgement of the AFAF did not appear in the Aldeburgh Festival Programme Book until 1974 – the year Betty Randolph Bean, known to Britten and Pears through her work for the New York office of the music publishing house Boosey & Hawkes, was appointed to the Board. The AFAF was not granted Tax Exempt Status until 1978 but serious fundraising for the School had started during 1975.

The members of the Board disagreed about the structure of the American Friends from the start. Francis Mason believed that there should be an American administrator in London and a British administrator in New York and he was keen to appoint David Lloyd Jacob (who later did join the Board) in the latter role. The idea was never put into effect and the only official appointment, apart from the usual officers, was made when Betty Bean, the Executive Vice-President, literally a larger-than-life figure and well known in New York musical circles, was appointed Fundraiser and Press and Publicity Officer.

From the start of her official association with Aldeburgh there were acrimonious disagreements over her salary and expenses, and endless complaints, directed at what might have seemed from across the Atlantic a laid-back administration in Aldeburgh, over lack of information and a perceived lack of co-operation. Bean was typically furious when, in 1980, a year after the School building had been opened, there was a small, low-key ceremony to acknowledge the support of the AFAF and a commemorative plaque was unveiled in the Seminar Room. The only names on the plaque are those of Alice Tully and Frank Taplin. She was incensed that not only were others missing but that the event had received no publicity: 'Where were the Press? Why was there nobody from the American Embassy?' she wrote to William Servaes.

Bean visited the Festival every year and she was very active and successful in raising funds for student scholarships, a fact that was acknowledged by both the administration and Pears personally, who between them agreed to share the payment of her salary and her expenses. (This had previously been a source of irritation to both Bean and the administration.) Sir Eugene Melville wrote to her in 1978, 'You, dear Betty, have done a most wonderful job for us and you deserve all the gratitude we can express.' At the same time and in the same file, there is the following comment: 'Betty Bean is a remarkable fund-raising success offset by remarkable expenditure and

© *Nigel Luckhurst*

Peter Pears and Alice Tully toast the unveiling of the AFAF plaque, 1979

As an observer one is allowed a remarkable insight and a rare opportunity to see and to hear the phenomenal artistic development, vocally and musically, in the sixteen-to-twenty young artists privileged to partake in these sessions . . . The American Friends of the Aldeburgh Festival and the Canadian Aldeburgh Foundation can indeed be proud of their major contribution in providing facilities and scholarship aid to this important extension of the Aldeburgh activities which offers a unique opportunity to young artists from the United States and Canada.

REPORT TO THE BOARD OF THE AFAF
BY AN ANONYMOUS OBSERVER AT THE 1979 COURSES

has a touch of megalomania.' These disagreements certainly occurred but they are by no means the whole picture; Betty Bean was an enthusiastic supporter of all the activities at Aldeburgh; she had a warm personality and she showed great kindness and friendship to members of the School staff whenever they visited the United States.

The tensions between Aldeburgh and New York continued and they cannot all be accounted for by the disagreements between Betty Bean and the Aldeburgh administration. There was American resentment over seemingly interminable requests for financial support and there was annoyance in Aldeburgh over what were seen as endless complaints and demands. There were also disagreements over student travel expenses, particularly for string quartets who wanted to study at Snape.

William Servaes, accompanied by his wife Pat, undertook two visits to New York in an attempt to pour oil on rather troubled waters, but the mismatch of expectations each organization had of the other finally appeared unresolvable.

In 1982, in order to boost their fund-raising campaign, the AFAF appointed a professional fundraiser, Carole Southall. She was sent on a visit to Aldeburgh to familiarize herself with activities of the School and everyone was amazed and amused by her huge and likeable personality. But the methods of a New York fundraiser and Aldeburgh did not make a perfect match; additionally she did not see eye to eye with the rather stuffy Board of the AFAF and the appointment came to an end after a relatively short period – but she remains a good friend of all the members of staff who knew her.

Despite the difficulties, the AFAF did give substantial and generous support to the School, raising funds for student bursaries. In 1979 the first twelve American students funded by the AFAF arrived at Snape to study in the new School building. These singers and string players were: Elizabeth Anderson, Stanley Cornett, Gail Czajkowski, Melvin Earl-Brown, David George, Sharon Leventhal, Robert Puleo, Kari-Lise Ravnan, Douglas Robinson, Joseph Tambornino, Richard Ullman and Andrew Yarosh.

Melvin Earl-Brown was an extremely large, African American counter-tenor who had been accepted for several of the courses in 1979. When he walked into the Recital Room to perform in an end-of-course concert, Galina Vishnevskaya turned to a companion and said confidently in her broken English, 'Is basso.' When he started to sing she changed her mind and said, 'Is woman.' Earl-Brown became a great favourite and returned to the School the following year. In September 1980 he auditioned for Mstislav Rostropovich and made his US debut with the National Symphony Orchestra in a gala concert alongside Leonard Bernstein, Jean-Pierre Rampal and Isaac Stern. He went on to have a very successful career which was sadly cut short by his death at a very early age.

The Canadian Aldeburgh Foundation

The story of the Canadian Aldeburgh Foundation is very different. It was formed in 1975, later than the AFAF, with the elegant, charming Frenchwoman Françoise Sutton as its first President. She was married to Marshall Sutton, who, until his death in 2000, was a lifelong and much valued supporter of the Aldeburgh Festival. They both became close, personal friends of Pears. Her account of the origins of the Canadian Aldeburgh Foundation follows on pp. 54–5.

In 1976 Pears went to Toronto to give a fundraising concert that gave a great boost to the CAF. In the *Toronto Globe & Mail* of 12 November 1976 John Fraser wrote, 'Peter Pears, the great English tenor, whose thirty-year friendship and musical collaboration with composer Benjamin Britten has been responsible for some of the most exciting and sublime music created this century, is in Canada for the next ten days to take part in a series of concerts and masterclasses. On Sunday evening at the Edward Johnson Building, Torontonians will have a chance to hear him, accompanied by the eminent Welsh harpist, Osian Ellis, in a special concert to aid the Canadian Aldeburgh Foundation.

'On this visit Peter Pears said, "The Festival is secure, thank God. The big push now is to get the study centre at Aldeburgh properly established. It's Ben's greatest wish to see this done, although lately he's not been able to do much about it and so Imogen [Holst] and I are scuttling about here and there to do

Continued on page 56

I was a member of the Toronto Women's Musical Club which organized and presented concerts for music lovers in the city. I became the Concert Convenor and it was my job to choose the performers and to arrange the concerts, so I was always reading as much as I could, not only about festivals, concerts and performers in Canada and the United States but in Europe too. I needed to know as much as possible and, of course, I had read a lot about the Aldeburgh Festival, so one day in 1970 I said to Marshall, my husband, that I thought we should go to Aldeburgh and check it out.

We stayed at the Wentworth Hotel and we chose it because I knew that Kathleen Ferrier had stayed there and I thought that if it was good enough for Kathleen Ferrier it would be good enough for us. On that first visit we had great difficulty finding the Concert Hall at Snape. There seemed to be no road signs and certainly no signs to the actual hall; there was no evidence that some of the greatest music in the world would be performed there. It was all so understated. Eventually, after a search, we found the Maltings and attended a performance of The Rape of Lucretia *with Peter Pears, Janet Baker and John Shirley-Quirk. What an experience! We also went to a concert, 'Artist's Choice', in the Jubilee Hall with Cecil Aronowitz accompanied by his wife Nicola Grunberg in the first half. In the second half Cecil played Britten's* Lachrymae *accompanied by the composer and although Nicola Grunberg is a very fine pianist, to hear Britten at the piano was absolutely extraordinary and I cannot describe my feelings when I heard him play. I had never in my life heard such sounds. It was unforgettable.*

As far as the whole Aldeburgh experience was concerned, it was absolutely love at first sight and we returned to Aldeburgh every year for over twenty years. Of course, on that first visit we knew nobody there but by going so regularly we began to recognize and to talk to various other visitors to the Festival, including Nicholas Goldschmidt, who was the founder of the Vancouver Festival. We met Charles and Letty Gifford at Niki and Shelagh Goldschmidt's house in Toronto and it was there that the seed of the Canadian Aldeburgh Foundation was sown. [Charles Gifford was then the Treasurer of the Aldeburgh Festival and Letty, his wife, the amazing woman who single-handedly saved, refurbished and very successfully ran the Aldeburgh Cinema for many years.]

The Giffords invited us to stay with them for the 1975 Aldeburgh Festival. This was the year that we first met Ben and Peter. Ben was very ill at the time but, of course, we were thrilled to meet them. The Spenders – Sir Stephen and his wife – were also guests of the Giffords and one day we were all going to lunch. I was sitting next to Charles in the car and he produced out of his briefcase a file containing an 18-page document entitled 'The Incorporation of the Canadian Aldeburgh Foundaton'.

I was astonished but we took it back with us and Marshall and I tried to digest it. Marshall said to me, 'You can run it', and I thought, 'Can I?' 'Well, you'll never know until you try.' I had some experience of boards and administration as I had been President of the Women's Musical Club of Toronto but I had no knowledge of fundraising. Still, I agreed to take it on.

We had discussions with Charles and he told me that the first thing would be to establish a board and to appoint a vice-president. Charles said, 'I'll telephone Arnold Smith.' He was a Canadian diplomat and Commonwealth Secretary-General. Arnold Smith answered the telephone and Charles said, 'Françoise Sutton would like to speak to you.' I heard myself asking Arnold Smith, whom I had never met, whether he would become our vice-president. He agreed and I was very grateful but I did not actually meet him for another ten years and it was some time before I realized that all he was really agreeing to was to have his name on the letterhead – which we didn't have and couldn't afford!

Back in Toronto I set about forming a board and trying to find the money that would be absolutely essential. We invited Terry Sweeney, a lawyer, to join us, also the British Consul-General, McCartney Samples, and Bernard Ness, a business-man and a generous supporter of the arts. Marshall put $100 into our account, I put in $100 and so did Terry. Well, we had $300 – so we could begin. The first thing I did was to get a rubber stamp which we would use until we could afford letter-head. But the Canadian Aldeburgh Foundation had started and we worked from my little office.

Of course, the first priority was to raise funds but it was extremely difficult. The name Aldeburgh meant absolutely nothing to most people in Canada and Ben and Peter were known only in the musical world. The stock question was: 'Why should we give you money which will go abroad?' I would reply that it would be given to Canadians to go and study abroad and then return to Canada, but I'm afraid that most were not convinced. Luckily at this time John Fraser of the Toronto Globe & Mail *visited the Norwich Festival and had gone on to Aldeburgh; on his return to Toronto he wrote an extremely enthusiastic account of his visit and Terry and I invited him to lunch. We told him of our plans and he said he would help. Almost immediately he introduced us to the Amy Stewart Maclean Foundation who generously promised to fund us with $5000 for four years. We were off!*

We were also given funding ($500) from Canadian Esso and from the Ivey Foundation ($500), although not every approach was as successful. By 2008 we had given away over $300,000 in bursaries to Canadian students.

FRANÇOISE SUTTON

FIRST PRESIDENT OF THE CANADIAN ALDEBURGH FOUNDATION

© Nigel Luckhurst

Françoise Sutton, President of the Canadian Aldeburgh Foundation, unveils a plaque at the School commemorating the organization.

the job." The centre Pears is working to establish permanently is to be a home for students of stringed instruments and singing from all over the world and he is particularly keen on having a Canadian contingent. So is the Canadian Aldeburgh Foundation, which under its President, Françoise Sutton, is in the midst of a campaign to raise funds to send Canadian students to the centre.'

The piece by Fraser ends with a quote from Pears: 'All performances are fleeting. That's their nature and when something is particularly beautiful in performance, isn't the memory a happier place for a lodging than some canister of celluloid? Of course, we all use recordings and video equipment, but that doesn't change the fact that the mad pursuit to try and arrest this fleetingness is a mistake. An arrogant mistake.'

During this Canadian visit Britten was gravely ill and Pears was very anxious and distressed. He conscientiously continued with the concerts but finally an emergency call came from Sue Phipps to Françoise Sutton at home in Toronto while Pears was due to sing Britten's *Saint Nicolas* in Montreal. Sutton flew to Montreal, arriving at the Ritz Hotel just as Pears was leaving for the concert at Notre Dame Basilica. The concert organizers agreed to reverse the order of the works in the concert, thus allowing Pears to leave at the interval so that Sutton could whisk him away to the airport and he could catch the midnight plane to the UK. All those who were there still talk about Pears's consummate professionalism in insisting on performing.

Britten lived for only another fortnight after Pears's return, dying on 4 December 1976. A year later, on 16 November 1977, William Littler in the *Toronto Star* wrote about a further visit by Pears: 'When Benjamin Britten died last year, England's Aldeburgh Festival lost its guiding spirit but not its will to continue in the service of music . . . Aldeburgh has become a kind of Mecca for musicians, a place to study and play where the very air seems musical . . . Pears was in Toronto this week auditioning two dozen Canadian singers for the masterclasses he gives each year in the picturesque English coastal village. He also attended a concert at Massey College presented by the Canadian Aldeburgh Foundation at which the young Canadian musicians who attended this year's masterclasses performed before an invited audience. The Foundation exists in order to give such musicians the chance to study and perform in the very special atmosphere that is Aldeburgh. Without exception, this first group returned raving about the experience. In Pears's words, "They did Toronto proud." In their words, Aldeburgh reciprocated.'

Many Canadian students applied for both the Song and String courses and the Snape experience was to have a profound influence on their careers. Although he was not funded directly by the CAF, as he was already studying at the Royal College of Music in London, one of the Canadians who studied at the School was Gerald Finley, who had a part in an RCM production of Handel's *Rinaldo* with Basil Coleman as its director. Coleman was due to direct *Rodelinda* by the same composer for the School at Snape in 1985 and he suggested that Finley should come and sing for him and for Steuart Bedford. 'To sing for these two amazingly high-profile people was a complete gift and I was thrilled.' Describing that time, he says that it was the beauty of the Suffolk environment, the wide skies, the beach at Aldeburgh and the marshes at Snape, combined with an atmosphere where the only thing that mattered was the music, that made it 'an incredibly precious experience'.

As a student at the College he was committed to the programme there and like so many others studying at various conservatories he often found it very hard to juggle those commitments with the courses at Snape. 'When the brochure came and one saw all the absolutely amazing people who were going to teach, one just thought, how many of these can I do? And will I be fortunate enough to get on a course?'

In 1986, after a furious bout of that very juggling, Gerald Finley was selected for the *Così fan tutte* course, which was directed by Murray Perahia and which was, in many ways, a watershed for the School.

Shortly before rehearsals with the orchestra were due to start, Perahia decided that he would not conduct the performances himself and handed over to Ivor Bolton. This was Perahia's first experience of overseeing the musical preparation of an opera and he felt that he did not have the right experience for the recitatives. Finley says, 'We were all absolutely devastated but it made me realize how great he was and how completely without vanity. He felt that the music deserved the

© Sim Canetty-Clarke

Gerald Finley

very best and he felt that he was not able to give it that very best. It was a combination of true humility and greatness.'

Finley also had sessions with Pears and his clearest memory is of Pears teaching him 'never to forget the sweetness of the words; they are the wings of communication. We all have our own unique voice and everyone has his own unique way of communication but the music takes it into a new language.' When Finley first sang for Pears, he said, 'I'm afraid it's just something very straightforward', and Pears replied, 'My dear, nothing is just straightforward. We can always make it into something extra and special.'

Gerald Finley went on to the National Opera School and then joined the Glyndebourne Chorus. From there his career went from strength to strength and he is now one of the most celebrated baritones in the world, singing in the inaugural production at the new Glyndebourne Opera House of *Le nozze di Figaro*.

Although they were never involved in the Opera courses, the two mainstays of so many of the Song courses were the Canadian pianists Stephen Ralls and Bruce Ubukata, both now resident in Toronto. Stephen Ralls was born in the UK and had first been involved with Britten and Pears through the English Opera Group. In 1978 he went to Toronto to join the staff of the Opera School (which he eventually directed). Bruce Ubukata is from Ontario. They played for Song courses every single year from 1974 until 1993, an astonishing nineteen years of unbroken commitment.

Ralls was greatly loved and admired by the students. He is a very fine pianist, a quiet man and very modest, with profound knowledge of the repertoire. The students were always able to benefit from his advice; working with him undoubtedly helped them to gain as much as possible from the masterclasses.

Stephen Ralls and Bruce Ubukata became close friends of Nancy Evans and Eric Crozier and there were many dinners where the conversation sparkled and everyone was relaxed and happy. Often Nancy Evans had worked at the School all day and would then come home and cook dinner for her guests – her favourite *pollo a la catalana*. 'It was unrelenting toil with a light touch,' Ubukata said. 'We just adored her.'

Ralls and Ubukata became a part of Aldeburgh life and Aldeburgh became a very real and important part of their lives. 'Aldeburgh informed my whole life and changed it,' Ubukata said. 'When I first went there and experienced that English setting, a part of me felt that I was coming home. We were so warmly welcomed and we were so lucky to be there in the company of all those great musical figures. Peter's fondness for Canada made a difference, of course, and we can now reflect on the disproportionate influence that the School had on musical life in Canada – and continues to do so.

' I shall never forget the volunteers who helped at the School and who were crucial to the atmosphere of the place. They were so involved and had such extraordinary links with the people that we were venerating. I remember Peter du Sautoy [a member of the Aldeburgh Foundation Board and later

The School was unique in that it provided the link between the conservatoire and the profession; there was nothing else quite like it. The courses were the perfect length because although one could be solitary there was sufficient time for bonding with the other students, so although it was all very serious, there was also an awful lot of fun. One became part of a family. I shall never forget the practice rooms at the School where there were no distractions; there was a complete love of making music and nothing else mattered. One of the things that the students learned there, and certainly something that I learned there, was that it was completely up to you, you had to take complete responsibility for what was happening and for what came next.

It was not only that we were being taught by such stars but that they were willing to share so much with us that made it all such a treasure. The students felt supported all the time and everything possible was done to help them. The bursaries were so important and it was wonderful for the students to have the financial worries taken away from them so that they could concentrate entirely on the work. We were not only turned into better musicians but into better people.

GERALD FINLEY

Portrait of Mollie and Peter du Sautoy by Max Chapman

Deputy Chairman] and Mollie, his wife, attending the classes and Mollie arranging the flowers on the hall table in the School. And I remember how impressed I was by Mollie and others going from door to door in Aldeburgh to drop in leaflets about School concerts. It was certainly not a spectator sport for them.' (Mollie du Sautoy, a very good pianist herself, had been a personal friend of Britten since the 1930s.) Ubukata remembers one occasion that he and Ralls went to dinner with the du Sautoys and he noticed in the hall a painting by David Milne, a Canadian artist. 'Oh yes,' Mollie du Sautoy said. 'That was a wedding present from Vincent Massey.' (The Right Honourable Vincent Massey had been the Governor-General of Canada.)

Bruce Ubukata laughed about the formidable Aldeburgh landladies who accommodated the students and remembers particularly the reactions of the North American students to this aspect of English life. One very doughty girl, having got wet through in a storm, was told in a kindly manner by her landlady that she should have a hot bath: 'There was only about two inches of hot water and then it ran cold but I knew that she could hear me and I was so afraid of her disapproval that I actually got into this dreadful cool bath and splashed about.' And another very fine New York baritone was utterly amazed to be given what he described as 'fish' for breakfast: 'She gave me *fish* for breakfast!' Ubukata had to explain that to the English, kedgeree is a highly prized breakfast dish. It is rather typical of Aldeburgh that another rather eccentric landlady surprised her North American guest by announcing that she was collecting all the fish bones she could find to make into copies of Anglo-Saxon jewellery.

For Ralls and Ubukata, it was Pears who was the pinnacle of the experience: 'He was so protective of the students,' Bruce Ubukata said, 'and so genuinely cared for their welfare, which was such a measure of the man. He was a great figure and we were lucky to be in his presence.'

When Gerhard Hüsch came to the School to give a series of classes, there was considerable tension between him and Pears. He lectured Pears relentlessly on every subject, including his diet, which Pears found very tedious and which he totally ignored. Everybody there was aware of this tension and Ralls and Ubukata remember it very well. An additional cause for strain was Hüsch's belief that every word that passed between teacher and student should be heard by everybody present and Pears's belief that some things should be kept private. On one occasion, exasperated by a student's performance, Hüsch said, 'It's as if I have never worked with you on this song.'

'Well, I have,' Peter chipped in. 'Well done, James.'

In a letter to Graham Johnson at the time, Pears wrote, 'The recipe for study is a good one, I think, and if the student is sensitive and can take the furious pace, he or she will never be the same again . . . quite!'

During the early 1980s, the School building was given over to the interminable Official Enquiry into the advisability of building a second nuclear power station on the coast north of Aldeburgh, 'Sizewell B'. The Enquiry meant a useful income,

© Nigel Luckhurst

Stephen Ralls playing the Maltings piano during a 1977 course, with Bruce Ubukata turning pages

Galina Vishnevskaya

particularly when it overran its original schedule. However, many of the masterclasses had to be relocated as a result to the private houses of local, and supportive, residents.

Galina Vishnevskaya started giving masterclasses in Russian Song in 1981 and Ralls and Ubukata were the accompanists for the great majority of her classes, including those held in the drawing room of Hugo and Margaret Herbert-Jones's house during the Sizewell B Enquiry. 'There was an E. F. Benson quality to it all,' Bruce Ubukata remembers, 'a typical Aldeburgh drawing room into which everyone was crowded and this great, exotic diva teaching.'

Pears wrote enthusiastically to Humphrey Burton, 'I must tell you. We have just had a week of Master Classes on Russian songs from Galina Vishnevskaya – the first she has ever done – Absolutely terrific, wildly exciting and adored by the singers – very practical, not a moment wasted [. . .] You really must have her on TV. Why not from the BP School? Everyone was mad about her. This week we have E. Schwarzkopf – very different. We hope to have them both next Summer again.'

It is interesting that Pears should have suggested televising Vishnevskaya's masterclasses. Looking back, Burton comments, 'I can't now remember why it never happened, particularly as masterclasses were of so much interest at that time and we televised others.'

Mstislav Rostropovich was famously impulsive, particularly when it came to political gestures in support of his friends or of ideas he cared passionately about. As the Berlin Wall came down, he flew into Berlin and was photographed playing his cello beside the Wall surrounded by joyful crowds.

Stephen Ralls and Bruce Ubukata were with Vishnevskaya the day after Rostropovich flew to Moscow at the time of the Yeltsin coup in 1993 without knowing who was behind the coup or how it would progress. At a dinner in the Red House Vishnevskaya told them she had had no idea that Rostropovich was going to Moscow until one of her daughters telephoned and said, 'Papa has flown to Moscow.' With a mixture of exasperation and pride Vishnevskaya said, 'Stupid Slava.'

Ralls says, 'It was an incredibly brave action; nobody knew how it would turn out and Slava ran a very real risk of being arrested. Galina was horrified that he had gone and had spent twenty-four hours of intense anxiety, but she told the story with admiration mixed with a degree of irritation.'

There were many lunch parties at Cherry House, the Aldeburgh home of Vishnevskaya and Rostropovich and she filled it to overflowing with guests and family; she loved to entertain in a very Russian way. Rita Thomson had been Britten's nurse, first at the National Heart Hospital, where, as a senior theatre nurse, she cared for him at the time of his operation in 1973, and later at the Red House. After Britten's death she had continued to live there as close friend of and companion to Peter Pears. She would often come to lunch, bringing Boysie the Red House dog along with her. Boysie was in the habit of leaping into Pears's lap and singing along with him. Pears would say, 'Poor Boysie, he tries so hard to sing in tune.'

Boysie joining Peter Pears in a duet

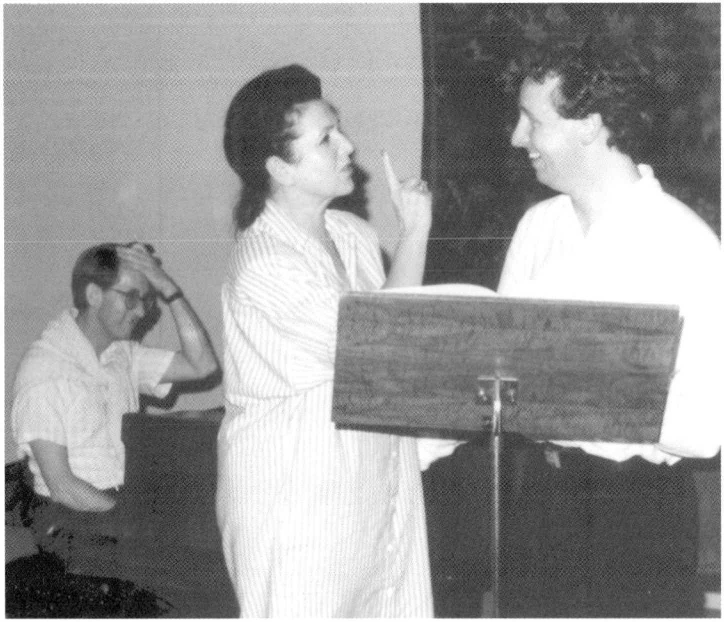

Above and opposite: Galina Vishnevskaya teaching Hugh Mackey with Stephen Ralls accompanying

Galina [Vishnevskaya] was a sorceress, with magic powers. When you were playing, if she wanted to stop you, she would just place the tip of her little finger very lightly on to the tip of your little finger and you could just feel the electricity.

BRUCE UBUKATA

Whenever Vishnevskaya sang, Boysie would jump on to her lap, throw back his head and start singing. Boysie had also sung with Suzanne Danco and Ileana Cotrubas. Rita Thomson remarks that Boysie's singing career included duets with some of the most famous singers in the world.

The contrast between the world of this flamboyant Russian, a former star of the Bolshoi Opera, and the small Suffolk town that is Aldeburgh was astonishing but somehow entirely in tune with the unique atmosphere of the School and Festival, where the presence of such exotic musical celebrities became simply a natural part of everyday life, accepted by visitors and by the people of the town.

It was in Aldeburgh that Vishnevskaya wrote the major part of her enormously successful autobiography, *Galina*. When she was driven to the School for her afternoon classes, if asked what she had been doing, she would reply, in her heavy accent, 'I write, I write. I tear up, I tear up.' On one unforgettable occasion before the book was published, at dinner in a pub in Easton, she was asked, 'Where actually were you during the war, Galina?' For the next half an hour, with her eyes flashing and with great emotion, she described the siege of Leningrad from the point of view of a young girl, living at first with her grandmother and then entirely alone during those unimaginably horrific days.

Another Aldeburgh star who became a great friend of Stephen Ralls and Bruce Ubukata was Joan Cross; they both remember her with tremendous affection and admiration.

Cross had had considerable experience of working with young singers, both at the National Opera School, which she had founded with Anne Wood in 1948, and then, in the 1960s, at the London Opera Centre. She lived for many years at Great Glemham and then, after her retirement, in Garrett House, Aldeburgh, where Ralls and Ubukata used to visit her and take her out to lunch so that she could enjoy her favourite steak-and-kidney pudding.

There were many Canadian singing students in the early days of the School, including Catherine Robbin, a winner of the Benson & Hedges competition; Jane Leslie MacKenzie, who became a special protégé of the Canadian Aldeburgh Foundation and whose career it particularly nurtured; James McLean, Ingemar Korjus, Henry Ingram and two who were to reach stardom, Adrianne Pieczonka and Michael Schade.

Henry Ingram's impressions of Suffolk (see p. 16) are probably typical of the reactions of the North American students who were inspired by the School. Janet Stubbs was another Canadian singer who attended masterclasses at Snape and who was very well thought of by Peter Pears. She valued her experiences at Snape but she has negative feelings about the actual masterclass format, which she thinks could be very destructive. Certainly it can be a very intimidating experience and some teachers are notably much gentler than others. Former students invariably talk of Pears's kindness and understanding of the difficulties they faced but they were often confronted by those who could be harsh and impatient. It was

We seemed to have the oldest living authority on any musical genre! There was Hugues Cuénod, Elisabeth Schwarzkopf, Hans Hotter, Gerhard Hüsch, and Frederick Fuller. But, of course, it was Peter who was the linchpin and, by giving so tremendously of himself, he gave the School its particular personality. I think that the School was somewhat like a blank canvas on which the visiting teachers could make their own impression and that encouraged and helped study; it wasn't throbbing with its own character.

STEPHEN RALLS

Nancy Evans was the lifeblood of the place, with that charm, that amazing presence and the considerable mettle. She didn't suffer fools gladly. And there was Eric [Crozier] who gave lectures and whose literary knowledge was an eye opener for so many of the students. Nancy supported Peter in a way that no one else could have and I remember seeing them one day listening to a class and just sitting quietly there together holding hands.

BRUCE UBUKATA

interesting to observe the different reactions of students: some picked themselves up after the tears and the depression and went on to benefit from the experience, while others were not able to do so. It is a very tough profession that they are hoping to enter and, as Roger Vignoles remarks, if they are not good enough, it is better that they recognize their limitations earlier rather than later.

The Canadian Cultural Counsellor at this period was David Peacock and it is difficult to imagine the Canadian Government being better served. He was conscientious to a remarkable degree and if there were any Canadians on a course he always came to Snape, to observe a masterclass or to attend the students' concert. He took an informed interest in their careers and was always ready with encouragement and practical advice.

Over a period the School and the Foundation sent representatives to the United States and to Canada in an attempt to encourage fundraising and, in the case of the American Friends, to try to sort out some of the misunderstandings. The first of these visits was initiated by the Boston branch of the English Speaking Union, who independently funded students at the School and whose Chairman, James Lawrence, was an enthusiastic supporter of all the School's activities. A professionally prepared slide show was shown to audiences in New York, Boston and Toronto. There were problems with variations in electric current in each city and showing the slides was a nail-biting experience.

The String Quartet courses were very influential on another Canadian string player and conductor, Ivars Taurins, who founded the Tafelmusik Baroque Orchestra and Chamber Choir in 1981. While studying at the University of Western Ontario he was a member of the North Western Quartet and they attended courses at Snape in 1977 and 1978.

The Canadian Aldeburgh Foundation continued to give the School its stalwart support and still does so today under its President Catherine Robbin and its Secretary-Treasurer Susan Wilson, another former student of the Britten–Pears School in its early days, who is responsible for the day-to-day running of the organization.

Thanks to Stephen Ralls and Bruce Ubukata the Aldeburgh link remains as strong as ever. They have for twenty-eight years organized a very popular annual series of concerts, 'The Aldeburgh Connection', showcasing singers who have studied at Snape and bringing to Toronto audiences the very best and most talented young artists who have benefited from the masterclasses.

Most of the leading Canadian singers have performed, and continue to perform, with the Aldeburgh Connection including (among Britten–Pears School alumni) Colin Ainsworth, Michael Colvin, Gerald Finley, Virginia Hatfield, James McLean, Adrianne Pieczonka, Catherine Robbin, Michael Schade, James Westman and Monica Whicher. There are frequent broadcasts and a number of Aldeburgh Connection CDs have been issued. The Aldeburgh Connection is

Studying at Snape 100 per cent influenced my whole career. We were a self-made quartet who just wanted to make music together and none of us had any experience of British or European culture. To be taught by such people as William Pleeth and Cecil Aronowitz was for us a sort of dream; we couldn't believe that we were actually going to have contact with these fabulous musicians. In Canada – and elsewhere – the push in the conservatories was all on a solo career; orchestral and chamber music were considered secondary to a solo career and the idea of 'superstardom' pervaded all the conservatories and, of course, does not allow you to concentrate on making music with others. My credo has always been on the importance of performing with others and of actually listening. So Snape provided us with a unique opportunity and access to the best teaching in the world. There was no school building then and we had classes all over the Maltings Concert Hall wherever a space could be found and I remember classes taking place in draughty little side rooms. But none of that mattered. The only thing that mattered was the teaching.

IVARS TAURINS

particularly proud of the fact that Peter Pears agreed to become Honorary Patron in 1982. Currently the Honorary Patrons include Steuart Bedford and Catherine Robbin.

The School certainly owes a huge debt of gratitude to both the American Friends of the Aldeburgh Festival and the Canadian Aldeburgh Foundation. Over the years both organizations have given such stalwart support to students from the United States and Canada who wanted to study at Snape and who would not have been able to do so without their generosity and hard work.

> *With the Aldeburgh Connection we sought to provide a performing milieu for the increasing number of singers who had studied at Aldeburgh, as well as engaging other young Canadian singers who were particularly adept in the art-song repertoire. A Sunday afternoon series was inaugurated in 1985 and continues to this day – these concerts are centred around musical, historical or literary themes and include narrative material, mostly drawn from documents of the relevant period. From time to time, we also present the more orthodox form of vocal recital, as seems appropriate.*
>
> STEPHEN RALLS

Even at this early stage, a family feeling engendered by the regular return of teaching staff was becoming a feature of life during the courses. Well before the School had its own 'home', a number of the teachers from previous years returned to offer courses in their specialist fields. They included in 1975 Hugues Cuenod and in 1976 Laura Sarti and John Shirley-Quirk. Morag Noble and Noelle Barker often assisted Nancy Evans in the regular morning Voice classes. It is hard to imagine anywhere else in the world where such a line-up could have been possible; although the classes were still held wherever a convenient space could be found and although they lasted for only a comparatively short period in the summer, the reputation of the School was growing throughout the musical world.

The regular accompanists, Graham Johnson and Roger Vignoles, Bruce Ubukata and Stephen Ralls, were joined later by Iain Burnside, Nancy Cooley, Jonathan Darlington, Jonathan Dove, Julius Drake, Malcolm Martineau and others equally distinguished. These pianists became the mainstay of the courses over many years and countless young singers and instrumentalists gained immeasurably from their advice and coaching.

String courses had been developing under the guidance of Cecil Aronowitz, a member of the Melos Ensemble and the English Chamber Orchestra, which at the time was virtually the Aldeburgh Festival's resident orchestra. His experience on the faculty at Banff in Canada and as Head of Strings at the Royal Northern College of Music enabled him to form a clear idea of how the String studies should develop. By the time of his death, following his collapse during a performance at the Snape Maltings Concert Hall in September 1978, he had established the String courses as an integral and essential part of the work of the School.

He was convinced that the establishment of a training orchestra was a very important way forward: 'a quite new idea, the formation of a professional orchestra (strings mainly) of advanced standard (mainly postgraduates) to train to take part in Aldeburgh events and to be promoted to the outside concert world'. He thought that by attracting gifted young players to work under great conductors the whole School would benefit and the String courses would flourish because so many of the orchestra would want to come and study at the School.

There was some anxiety that the formation of a training orchestra at Snape might conflict with the work of the BBC Training Orchestra in Bristol but it was eventually decided to combine it with the String Quartet courses; this allowed the Snape Maltings Training Orchestra (later the Britten–Pears Orchestra) to be formed, giving its first concert on 23 November 1975. Aronowitz invited the much sought-after teacher, William Pleeth, to join him. Pleeth, who had taught Jacqueline du Pré, and who had many international students, was to have a very long and distinguished association with the School and taught there every year until shortly before his death in 1999 at the age of eighty-three. Pleeth was greatly loved and admired by all his students.

In June 1976 Cecil Aronowitz directed a String Weekend devoted to baroque music and Mstislav Rostropovich gave a series of masterclasses. For the singers there were courses on Oratorio and Lieder. The School year ended with masterclasses for violin and viola given by Max Rostal.

Britten's death at the end of the year cast a long shadow but nevertheless acted as a spur to his friends and colleagues to ensure that his vision for the School was fulfilled.

One of the developments Britten had very much encouraged was the extension of String courses and in 1976 Aronowitz and Pleeth had discussed the idea of String Quartet courses. In 1977 the First International Academy of String Quartets was held at Snape; the teachers were Max Rostal, Erling Bengtsson, Cecil Aronowitz and William Pleeth. This was to become an annual event and the Second International Academy of String Quartets in 1978 was directed by Lorand Fenyves, Georges Janzer, Eva Czako and William Pleeth.

In 1979 the Amadeus Quartet directed the Quartet course. Among the students were the members of the Takács Quartet; the ensemble went straight from Aldeburgh to win the Portsmouth Quartet Competition. The String Quartet courses were soon an established success and continued to attract internationally distinguished quartets to teach young quartets from all over the world.

The year 1977 was an important one in the development of the School. Song, String and Academic courses were well subscribed and the reputation of the School as a centre of excellence was growing. The plans for the courses were becoming more ambitious and the vision of the future of the School as a unified structure was taking shape.

Peter Pears and Imogen Holst directed a two-week Bach course with George Malcolm (harpsichord) and Janet Craxton (oboe). There was a Handel course with Laura Sarti, John Shirley-Quirk and Winton Dean and a Schubert course with Thomas Hemsley. Imogen Holst and John Carol Case directed an English Song course.

After Aronowitz's death in 1978 Pears immediately invited Hugh Maguire to take over as Director of String Studies. At that time Maguire was at the very peak of his professional career, former leader of the London Symphony Orchestra, the BBC Symphony Orchestra and the Allegri Quartet, a member of the Melos Ensemble and with a successful solo career. Pierre Monteux had once said that Hugh Maguire was the best concertmaster he had ever worked with, not only because of his exceptional ability but because he had an intuitive understanding of the conductor's requirements.

Maguire had visited Snape many times at the invitation of Aronowitz, who was both a colleague and a friend, and says that he had fallen in love with the place and with the whole concept of the School. He says that when he received Pears's invitation he was so excited by the idea that he gave up many of his performance commitments in London without hesitation and moved to Suffolk as soon as he could to take up the new position.

Like Aronowitz, Maguire had his own personal contacts with very distinguished musicians. However, his was a slightly different vision for the development of the School. Despite the fact that the String Quartet courses had been taught by international players, Aronowitz had placed an emphasis on British teachers for the regular courses and British conductors for the orchestra. Maguire felt that although these guests were very distinguished, they were already available to teach British students in other institutions. He believed that the School should attract the best teachers and conductors from Europe and North America and that this would give students an opportunity they could get nowhere else within the UK.

As a consequence he started to invite the finest musicians from all over the world. He laughs as he remembers that some of them he didn't know personally at all – however, 'I wrote and they came.' Among the internationally famous string players that Maguire invited and who taught at the School during this period were Gérard Caussé, Pierre Fournier, Josef Gingold, Bruno Giuranna, Franco Gulli, William Primrose, Ruggiero Ricci, and the Beaux Arts Trio, who directed a Piano Trio course. The first person from the United States that he invited to conduct the Snape Maltings Training Orchestra was Alexander Schneider.

Maguire's initiative offered experiences for the players that went far beyond their normal expectations. There were always problems to overcome when trying to assemble the orchestra. The majority of the players were students at the various conservatories and while they always wanted to come to Snape and obviously derived benefit from the courses, it was often difficult for the conservatories to release them from their regular commitments. This resulted in hours and hours of persuading and cajoling on the part of the School staff as they tried to fix the orchestra for an SMTO course.

In 1979, Hugh Maguire and John Owen, then on the School staff and administering the String courses, put into place a new and very strict auditioning process. Maguire was determined that the orchestra would consist of only the best young players in the country. These auditions were held regularly, mainly in London. Maguire remembers this period with affection: 'They were wonderful days. Peter, John [Owen] and I were all going in the same direction and we were so precisely focused. We knew exactly what we wanted.'

Many of the Snape Maltings Training Orchestra players now talk of the tremendous effect that studying at Snape had on them. Life-long friendships were made. String quartets were formed, including the Brindisi Quartet whose members were all leaders of the SMTO sections.

Alexander Schneider was an extraordinary, charismatic man who had unique links with the great artists of the past. He had been a member of the legendary Budapest String Quartet and had been a very close friend of Pablo Casals. He had premiered many works by composers such as Stravinsky, of whom he was heard to say, 'That son of a bitch still owes me twenty-five dollars.'

Alexander Schneider and Hugh Maguire working with the strings of the Snape Maltings Training Orchestra in 1980. The rehearsal is being held in the former Working Men's Club, Thorpeness.

Douglas Boyd

> *Snape was extraordinary. It was so much more than just another music course; the spirit of Britten was there, we felt that he had bequeathed it to us and we were all so much aware of it.*
>
> DOUGLAS BOYD

Douglas Boyd, who was to become one of the founder members of the Chamber Orchestra of Europe and is now a very successful conductor, was the oboist in the early SMTO under Schneider. Schneider immediately recognized Boyd's exceptional talent and was so deeply impressed by it that, on his return to New York, he asked his manager, Frank Salomon, to write suggesting that Douglas Boyd should come to New York and study with him.

Boyd says that the experience of working with Schneider at Snape and in New York was a revelation: 'It was the extraordinary way that Sasha made music, his fantastic energy, the incredible joy of his phrasing, that made me realize that this is the way music should be. It was the way he shaped the music that was such an inspiration.'

After Boyd had been invited to go to New York, it was realized that there would be a problem with funding his trip. Just getting there in those days was expensive; this was long before the era of cheap international flights, but the funds to help Boyd to go to the United States were raised. Boyd worked with Schneider at his seminar and then, encouraged by Salomon, who was to become his manager as well as Schneider's, Boyd was persuaded to enter the Young Concert Artists Competition and was one of the prizewinners. (Another winner in the same competition was Dawn Upshaw.)

In 1981 the Chamber Orchestra of Europe was formed by Douglas Boyd and a group of fellow musicians, many of whom had been members of the SMTO with him or had played with him in the European Community Youth Orchestra. It soon established a world-wide reputation on the concert platform and in the recording studio, touring with, among other distinguished conductors, Alexander Schneider himself.

In conjunction with the Singers courses and String courses, Donald Mitchell, the musicologist, critic and publisher, devised regular Academic weekend courses and in the early years these were planned to extend and underpin the performing courses. As a result there was the opportunity for in-depth study of the composers whose works the students were performing. Later Academic courses covered a far wider area and subjects such as composition, film music, ethnomusicology and the works of contemporary composers were studied.

Over the years these courses began to fall into two separate categories: some were simply Academic weekends, unrelated to any particular performing course, while others were closely linked to the repertoire being studied at the School. All the Academic weekends were extremely popular and it was quite normal to have between forty and fifty students enrolled for a course. Those that were performance-related were very carefully designed to give the students an extra dimension to the masterclasses and to give them a more profound understanding of the repertoire and the composers or the musical genre on which they were working.

With Donald Mitchell as the Director of Academic Studies the faculty was guaranteed to be of the very highest calibre and the students were provided with unequalled opportunities for

The Brindisi String Quartet – Patrick Kiernan (second violin), Jacqueline Shave (leader), Robert Irvine (cello) and Katie Wilkinson (viola) – who met and first played together when leading their respective sections in the Snape Maltings Training Orchestra

serious study. The programme of courses was ground-breaking and entirely compatible with the high standards that were being set in every area of the School's life.

With Singers and String courses, the Training Orchestra and Academic courses all gradually developing and growing, the work of the School was beginning to fall into a regular annual pattern. In September 1977 the management of the Aldeburgh Festival–Snape Maltings Foundation produced a document that attempted to formulate the proposed future development of the School:

'Existing facilities for postgraduate musical studies are at best scanty. The Yehudi Menuhin School and Chetham's School cater only for young people of school age. The Royal College of Music and the Royal Academy offer some postgraduate training but this is not comparable to the highly selective studies already started at Snape. We believe that there is no other British school designed for the special needs of the very gifted. The fact that the courses already under way (which are planned to form the basis of the Britten–Pears School) are complementary to, rather than rivalling, those at the Royal College of Music, is perhaps demonstrated by the presence on the AF–SMF Council of the Director of the Royal College.

'We start, therefore, from the premise that there is a gap in the facilities available for developing the most talented young musicians during the period between leaving college and finding worthwhile work as a performer, and that a highly selective school such as that already started at Snape can play a key role in filling this gap. The courses are short and the numbers small, but it is intended to group the courses into continuous sequences. The teachers are drawn from all parts of the world and about half the students are from overseas. The arrangements of the courses and the selection of both teachers and pupils is highly flexible. The String Quartet course of September 1977 brought young ensembles from all parts of the world, offering teaching at a level which both students and the internationally known chamber music artists who taught agreed was far higher than could be found at major conservatories.'

In the same month Donald Mitchell issued a statement in which he said, 'If we were to bring together the practical element and the theoretical element as I understand it, that is, as an indispensable partner in the creation of living performance then I think we should be well on our way to the creation in our lives of a unique educational establishment [. . .] It must be plain to everybody inside and outside Snape that the presence of the archives, of the manuscripts, of the Britten–Pears Library, is of remarkable importance to the work of the School.' Writing of the importance of the academic combined with the highest level of performance in singing and string studies, he added, 'I think that we could have a quite stunning basis for a School that does not exist elsewhere in the United Kingdom and which might have a genuinely revolutionary effect on music-making and on the standards of musical performance in this country [. . .] It may well be that Aldeburgh is too remote to be an ideal place for a large college. But the environment is eminently suitable for concentrated study of a specialized nature. And the small size of the proposed school is a help in enabling the arrangement of courses to remain flexible and the choice of students discriminating.'

In February 1978, Dr Swinburne was still there, despite at least two attempts to resign, neither of which was accepted, and still producing memoranda about structures. In 1978 he issued a document entitled 'The Formative Period', which, after all that had gone before, says, somewhat surprisingly, 'The shape of the School should be held without a too rigid adherence to a detailed plan. The natural growth will itself find many of the paths we are looking for [. . .] The School exists to give the most advanced instruction to the most talented pupils [. . .] Provided what is done serves this purpose, in the long run it may be necessary to compromise here and there.'

All this time, while the School was in the first phase of its development, activity was all very much on a part-time basis and, indeed, this pattern has been followed ever since. Yet in 1978, only a year before the School building opened, a conference of the Gulbenkian Foundation was held to discuss the future of Music Education with both Marion Thorpe and Dr Swinburne attending. This meeting discussed and apparently agreed plans for the School to become a full-time educational institution that would apply for government funding, but what became of these plans is not clear; certainly they were not put into practice. There also existed at the time a vague plan for the School to become a part of the Colchester Institute, a sort of satellite of the Institute, but this, too, was never taken further, possibly as a result of Dr Swinburne's eventual departure.

The factor that was to make the School unique was that a view was emerging that all its activities should be part of a unified whole. The School was closely linked to an international Festival with consequent performance opportunities. The combination of courses for singers and string players, coupled with the existence of a training orchestra, made it possible for all these different strands to be brought together in fully staged opera performances. The existing Academic courses were designed to give students an opportunity for serious study and, at the same time, many of the practical courses were underpinned by lectures and seminars giving students a valuable opportunity to study in greater depth the composers and genres associated with their courses. There was also access to the Britten–Pears Library.

During all these years the vision of the School in its own building, its own home, had been very much in the minds of Britten and Pears. Everybody involved in the School knew that this was the ultimate aim and was essential if the School was to flourish, but the estimated costs were substantial and simply funding the courses was always a problem. All the courses ran at a deficit. The combined courses up to October 1974 showed a running deficit of £12,819 and an annual deficit of £11,000

© Nigel Luckhurst

The Britten–Pears School building in its original incarnation as a barley store

was forecast. In today's terms this would translate to a deficit of close on £100,000 each year.

Fundraising for the School had already started and an anonymous benefactor gave a donation of £2,000. William Servaes made an important contribution to the finances of the School by negotiating a generous sponsorship of the SMTO with Northern Star Insurance Group, but it was obvious that further large sums of money would be required if the School was to continue to grow and if hopes for a School building were to be realized. Britten's death was to provide a catalyst for the essential fundraising to fulfil his vision.

In order to help with fundraising for the School building, Marion Thorpe, Dame Janet Baker and Mstislav Rostropovich sent out the following letter: 'We would like to ask for your help over a project which is very close to our hearts.

'You know, of course, of the development of the Aldeburgh Festival over the last thirty years, the building of the Maltings Concert Hall at Snape and, most recently, the development of educational activities there. These activities have in fact been a pilot scheme towards a small but important School for Advanced Music Studies attached to the Concert Hall, and a statement setting out its objectives in more detail is enclosed.

'For the School to be properly effective adequate lecture and practice rooms are required, and these can be provided within the Concert Hall complex. The plans have already been drawn up and we have so far raised over £220,000 of the £500,000 required.

'The success of this project was one of Benjamin Britten's main preoccupations in the last years of his life, and as a memorial to him – and, indeed, as a tribute to the unique contribution both he and Peter Pears have made to the world of music – we feel that now is the time for their friends and admirers to make a concerted effort to provide what is needed.

'Five hundred donations of £500 would enable us to start work this year with a real chance of having the building, which we propose to name the Britten–Pears building, ready for use in October 1978.

'Will you please help forward this exciting project by providing or promising to raise at least one of the units of £500 required? Cheques should be made out to "Aldeburgh Festival–Snape Maltings Foundation Limited" and sent to us as soon as possible.

'We believe passionately that the advanced training which can be provided at Snape is vital to the musical life of this country and that the work done there will help to pass on to young artists the musical tradition established by Benjamin Britten and Peter Pears over the years.'

The fundraising campaign was sufficiently successful for Sir Eugene Melville to authorize Arup Associates to invite tenders for the building of the School in August 1977 and in October 1977 the decision to go ahead with the local firm of Haymills was taken with a very tight budget of £370,000. The School would be converted from what had been the grain store of the original maltings, adjoining the Concert Hall, taking in the germinating bay and forming the courtyard that was to become the artists' car park.

Although there was general fundraising for the project, without the extremely generous support of the Britten–Pears Foundation it is certain that the conversion would not have been possible and the funds would certainly not have been raised in such a short period of time. Support from the Vestey family should also be acknowledged. William Servaes's wife, Pat, was a devoted supporter of the arts; she was a member of the Vestey family and their contribution to the building of the School was very generous and significant.

Strangely, and sadly, it has to be said that this incredible achievement took place in an atmosphere of uncertain personal relationships. For some time surrounding these extraordinary musical activities there had always been a suggestion of what might be termed paranoia. Someone who worked in the administration at this time remembers, 'There was always such secrecy – nobody really trusted anyone else.' At no time could the ambience have been described as sunny, and it is hard to understand why this should have been the case. There was a lack of trust between the administration and the Red House, between the administration and the Trustees of the Britten–Pears Foundation, and between one individual and the next. Servaes was by nature suspicious and the prevailing mood had become ingrained within the organization.

It was curious: everyone involved shared the same aims and was committed to the future of the Festival and the vision for the School, and yet that underlying anxiety was ever present. Although no one would have described him- or herself as part of one big happy family, individual commitment to the vision for the School and its future was so strong that it was able to overcome these personal differences.

Central to that vision was the School building itself. After the fire in 1969, when the Concert Hall was rebuilt, a number of alterations had been made to the complex, including the addition of a flat for the caretaker. Arup had also been asked then to prepare a master plan for the whole site to include the conversion of the turning bays into a Recital Room. When the School was eventually built this is exactly how it was done, with very little change from the original master plan.

Derek Sugden, of Arup, so closely associated with the original conversion of the Maltings, was now equally involved in the conversion of the School. Sugden, who is one of the foremost acousticians in the world, and his wife, Jean, had been regular Festival visitors. Having been so closely involved with the original Concert Hall conversion, both he and his wife were well known to Britten and Pears and it was natural that he should have been consulted over the conversion of the School building. There is no one with greater knowledge and understanding of the building and the acoustics of the Concert Hall and the School.

Peter Foggo, also of Arup, was the architect. There were initial difficulties in this arrangement. Before he was appointed as General Manager of the Aldeburgh Festival–Snape Maltings

Foundation, William Servaes had been the Administrator for George Trew and Dunne, a firm of London architects, where John Trew was a partner. Servaes had appointed Trew as Secretary of the AF–SMF, and he was now keen that Trew should become the architect for the School, with Arup acting as consultants. Arup was not at all happy with this proposal and a lengthy correspondence ensued, culminating in a meeting between Sir Philip Dowson of Arup, Derek Sugden, William Servaes and the Countess of Cranbrook. Derek Sugden recalls that Fidelity Cranbrook called his letters on the subject 'somewhat Delphic'. The outcome of the meeting was that Peter Foggo was appointed the architect for the School and John Trew became the project manager.

Sugden talked about some of the problems that had to be overcome. He asked Pears exactly what the acoustic requirements for the proposed Recital Room would be and Pears replied, 'Oh, you know all about that sort of thing, Derek.'

'But, Peter, I must know exactly what you want.'

'Well, we want it for everything.'

Sugden also recalled a conversation he had had with Imogen Holst prior to the conversion of the Concert Hall.

Imogen Holst said, 'Mr Sugden, we want you to arrange for all the lovely sounds like birdsong to be heard and all the horrible sounds like aircraft to be excluded.'

'Miss Holst, you are asking me to defy the laws of physics.'

'But, Mr Sugden, we have engaged the clever people at Arup Associates.'

It was finally decided that the acoustic properties of the Recital Room must match those of the Concert Hall.

In 1980 (after the completion of the School) Tony Aldous, an environmental and architectural journalist wrote a piece for the *Illustrated London News* on the subject of Music Schools, comparing the work done on the Cambridge Music School with that at the Britten–Pears School:

'The Britten–Pears School at Snape, converted from maltings buildings to the south of the Concert Hall is very different from that at Cambridge. The budget was considerably tighter. It called for a rehearsal-cum-recital-cum-lecture room to be created out of the turning bays wing of the maltings [. . .] The requirements for the Recital Room were exacting. More intimate than the Concert Hall but with the same reverberation so that performers could be sure of comparable acoustics.

'The brief also asked for flexibility to seat 150 people for recitals and lectures, or have a clear floor for rehearsal work. This the architects, somewhat against their own judgement, provided by means of removable raked seating. The designers now accept that this was right, for the room is used much more frequently for public performances than was expected [. . .]

'The architects and their client learned several important lessons from the shortcomings of the first phase of the Maltings complex. The Concert Hall, for instance, has no thermal insulation in its roof and is expensively heated by electricity. Conversion of the building to the south into a music school had as a high priority the laying of insulating felt under the roof retiled with original and other second-hand pantiles and central heating from a new boiler house [. . .] The two buildings have this in common: they have both been built to tight budgets: both seek to combine the teaching of music with frequent public performances and both have achieved facilities and an atmosphere for both teaching and listening which should be an inspiration and a delight.'

Arup issued a report after the completion of the conversion of the School:

'Until 1965 these buildings were used as a store for new barley and the subsequent cleaning of it. The grain was stored until the malting season started in October in steeps of water on the courtyard side of the building and was then drained off and turned out on to the floor (where the Recital Room and Courtyard now are) before being taken into the Concert Hall building for drying. Thus the malthouse, which formed the kernel of the maltings complex of buildings, has been adapted very successfully to a totally different purpose and is a fine example of the flexibility of nineteenth-century industrial architecture.

'Although the outside remains exactly as it was built, except for new windows and the addition of an entrance porch, the inside has been completely gutted. Originally there were three upper floors of a primitive nature, supported by steel columns and beams. These had to be taken out stage by stage and replaced by two new floors. One of the problems that the architects had to solve was the need, in order to cut down on noise transference to provide as much "mass" as possible in each floor thickness without overloading the existing external walls and foundations. Hence the brick arches.

'The accommodation contained within the buildings that have just been converted for the School comprises:

'On the ground floor there is an Entrance Porch leading to the Entrance Hall and on the right there is the Reception and Registration Office, a Staff Office and the Faculty Room.

'To the left of the entrance there is the students' Common Room and Snack Bar, male and female lavatories, each with a shower. Outside and between the lavatories is a recess for a washing-machine and spin-dryer. (Students often have difficulty coping with their laundry in their lodgings.)

'Straight ahead in the Entrance foyer are two openings leading to the Recital Room. This room used to be the gallery and luckily the floor level is about five feet below the ground floor of the South Block. By using a system of sliding platforms this can easily be converted to an open space with a flat floor for orchestral rehearsals or a gallery. When the platforms are extended it becomes a Recital or Lecture Room seating 150. One of the requirements was that the Recital Room should have the same acoustics as the main Concert Hall when full, and this dictated the shape and form of the new roof.

'Between the two entrances to the Recital Room there is:

'The Projection Box and Lighting Control Box, and at the far end is a Chair Store with direct access to the main Concert Hall complex and the Caretaker's Office.

‘On the first floor there are six small Practice and two large Ensemble Practice Rooms, each separated by a storeroom or staircase to provide as much sound insulation as possible. (To provide total sound insulation was prohibitively expensive.) As it is much easier to damp down resonance than to add it in, all the surfaces are hard, i.e. maple strip flooring and plastered walls. Full-length curtains will be provided on the window walls so that the acoustics of each room can be individually adjusted. All the corridors and stairs are carpeted to reduce transmitted noise to a minimum.

‘On the second floor and at the east (river side) of the building is a further large Practice Room, making a total of three. Between the two staircases is the Seminar Room. This large room can be divided up into three main areas by movable screens and fittings providing a lecture area for up to 40 students and observers.

‘There is a Reading Room to be used as an adjunct to the Holst Library. This is run in conjunction with the Britten–Pears Library at the Red House. The stock of the Holst Library has been provided almost entirely by Miss Imogen Holst. It consists of many sets of vocal and instrumental parts, miniature scores, vocal scores of opera and oratorio, books on music and other subjects, reference books and a catalogue of reference books available for consultation in the Britten–Pears Library. An interesting feature of the Holst Library will be a permanent display of all the music by Gustav Holst which is in print.

Bookshelves in the Holst Library at the Britten–Pears School

'The Holst Library is primarily a lending library for tutors and students and will be the central point for the supply of music for the courses at the School. There will be a working arrangement between the Holst Library and the Britten–Pears Library for more advanced research to be done in the latter.

'A new Car Park has been built in the south-east corner of the site, which will take about 80 cars. There is easy access from this Car Park to the Promenade and Restaurant and South Bar entrances.'

After the School opened the successful operation of the retractable seating in the Recital Room depended entirely on the skills of Bob Ling, who from 1971 had been the Concert Hall Manager and who now took responsibility for the School building too; he was able to remove or put in place the raked seating in only thirty minutes, an astonishing achievement.

Bob Ling, a local man, had from the age of twelve been a maltster working at the Maltings. After being made redundant he became a milkman and then he and Doris, his wife, worked together as gravediggers. After the conversion of the Concert Hall, when Bob Ling was first engaged as caretaker, Doris was put in charge of cleaning. This remarkable couple were well known to musicians all over the world. They became an integral part of the whole operation, familiar with all the requirements for running an international concert hall and all the needs of the musicians who performed there, able to set the stage for any forces and completely unfazed by any of the challenges that were thrown at them.

Tea with Bob and Doris Ling was a part of daily life at the Maltings and there must be students and musicians all over the world who remember them with the utmost affection and who probably still laugh at Doris Ling's risqué jokes and stories. Bob Ling, for many years after he retired, led tours of the Maltings, delighting visitors with the depth of his knowledge, not only of the buildings but also, of course, of their history.

The external appearance of the School building was unchanged except for the replacement of the old timber windows with new double-glazed ones and the addition of the entrance porch (which has since been demolished), which was described as 'an elegant, spacious glazed porch big enough for a dozen people to sunbathe in'. There are no stories of any of the students actually sunbathing but they certainly sat around in the porch, gossiping, eating sandwiches or just waiting for the minibus to take them back to Aldeburgh.

'A School must be affected by the nature of the buildings in which it has to work,' a 1978 internal AF–SMF document has it. 'It is as yet too early to assess the practical qualities of the new teaching block, but there is reason for the liveliest hopes. Architects and craftsmen appear to have effected a conversion that compares not unfavourably with that of its neighbour, the Concert Hall.'

The work on the School was completed in December 1978, with remarkable speed. The final result was a building that achieved all its aims. The atmosphere produced by its neutral colours and simplicity of line, together with the excellence of its design and acoustics, worked precisely for its purpose, the serious study of music. The exterior still resembled an agricultural building of bare red brick, set among other rather battered agricultural buildings, but the impression as one walked into the foyer, decorated in subdued stone colours, with two doors into the Recital Room and a splendid specially commissioned limed oak table between them on which stood bronze busts of Benjamin Britten and Peter Pears, was that everything was exactly as it should be.

Pears lent the School a very fine tapestry to hang in the Recital Room and the permanent loan of a Steinway piano was made by Sir Eric and Lady Penn. The whole, finished building was a triumph for Arup, especially for Derek Sugden, as the acoustics matched the requirements so well; indeed, it was a triumph for everybody involved in its creation.

While the masterclasses held in the six years since the first classes for singers in 1972 had been successful and the work at Snape had gathered a growing reputation for excellence, everything had of necessity taken place in somewhat primitive surroundings. A dedicated School building was essential if cohesion and focus were to be achieved and when it was finally completed it surpassed all that could possibly have been imagined when the first tentative ideas for a school at Snape had been discussed in the early 1950s.

On 28 April 1979 the Britten–Pears School for Advanced Musical Studies was opened by Queen Elizabeth The Queen Mother, Patron of the Aldeburgh Festival:

© *Nigel Luckhurst*

HM Queen Elizabeth The Queen Mother is welcomed to the Britten–Pears School by Peter Pears. On the far right stands Sir Eugene Melville. The party is in the School's glass-sided porch, which has since being dismantled.

© Nigel Luckhurst

HM Queen Elizabeth The Queen Mother at the formal opening of the Britten–Pears School for Advanced Musical Studies on 28 April 1979. Peter Pears looks on; between them stand William Servaes and Sir Eugene Melville. To the right of Pears are Sir Eric and Lady Penn. Dr William Swinburne stands at the far right.

'I am delighted to be here today on an occasion which marks the fulfilment of the idea of Benjamin Britten and Peter Pears to set up a school of musical excellence at Snape.

'It is wonderful to know that the conversion of this splendid building has been made possible by the generosity of friends and admirers of Benjamin Britten, one of our country's greatest composers. It commemorates most fittingly his distinguished career and his devotion to the encouragement of young musicians and also his unique artistic partnership with Sir Peter Pears.

'Every thinking person will realize that the School must now stand at the beginning of a difficult course which will take an immense amount of thought, courage and sheer hard work to navigate successfully. But I have no doubt that the enthusiasm already sown will ensure that it will go from strength to strength.

'In congratulating everyone on what has been achieved so far, I extend to this exciting enterprise my very best wishes for the future.

'It now gives me great pleasure to open the Britten–Pears School for Advanced Musical Studies.'

Photograph courtesy of Arup

Previous page: The conversion nearing completion, with the porch to the left
Above and right: The entrance hall, with its distinctive curved brick roof
Facing: The Recital Room

Photographs courtesy of Arup

Above: The completed conversion showing the School building parallel to Snape Maltings Concert Hall

Left: The original construction of the roof

Facing: One of the rehearsal rooms on the second floor of the building

Photographs courtesy of Arup

Establishing a Routine: 1979–87

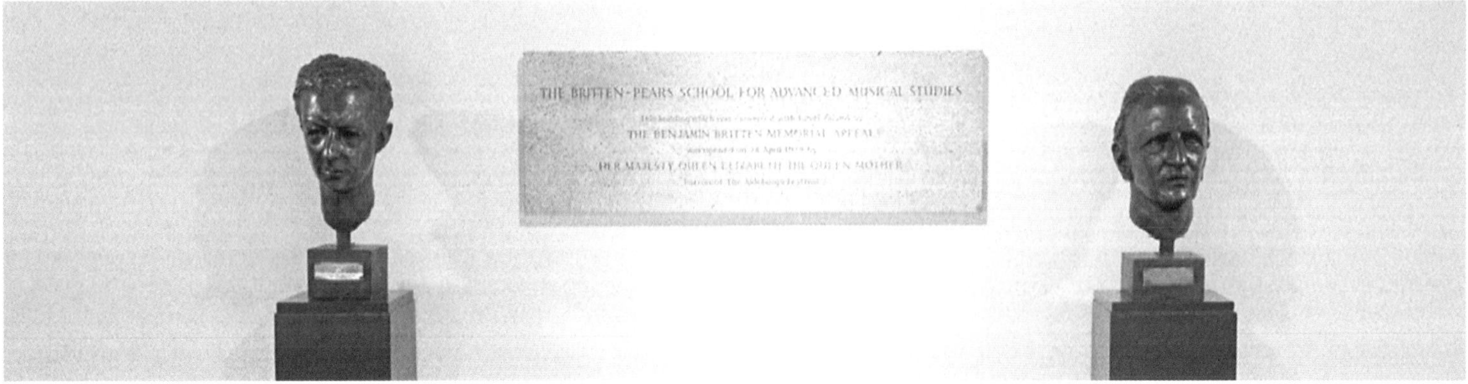

The School was now ready to operate in its own building and the first courses were due to start in July 1979. Two members of staff had been appointed in 1978: John Evans, who had been working at the Britten–Pears Library, and John Owen. For both this was their first job. John Evans was to be the Assistant to the Director of Singing Studies and John Owen the Assistant to the Director of String Studies.

I was the third member of staff, appointed in 1979, and I think my title was 'Administrative Assistant', which just about sums up the sort of dogsbody things that would have made up my job description – if there had ever been such a thing. I helped to arrange the catering, organized the transport schedules, drove people to and from Aldeburgh and mended the Tampax machine in the ladies' loos, which seemed to be broken on an almost daily basis.

My appointment had come about as a result of a conversation with William Servaes, who was known to everyone as 'Bill'. In April 1979 the 'Great Salmonella Scandal' had hit Aldeburgh. The Aldeburgh Festival–Snape Maltings Foundation ran a restaurant, called the Festival Club, on the ground floor behind its offices in the Suffolk Hotel on the High Street. The catering was undertaken by an Aldeburgh woman who was quite a good amateur cook and who had previously been a 'Dame' at Eton. Her food was pleasant enough but her methods could be a touch casual. She was in the habit of preparing the food at her house in the High Street, piling it into the back of her car and eventually transporting it down to the Club, without

© *Nigel Luckhurst*

John Owen (*left*) and John Evans (*right*) with Mstislav Rostropovich backstage at Snape Maltings Concert Hall

much attention being paid to 'Health and Safety'. For a time all went well.

One day in April, the weather might have become a little warmer and the chicken mayonnaise on the lunch menu would certainly not have passed close examination. The Club was fairly full and I was one of those who had the misfortune to eat the dish, with horrendous results. Seventy-nine of us went down with salmonella poisoning, some with comparatively mild symptoms but five of us came alarmingly close to death's door. The Club was closed immediately and Bill Servaes, nervous of the litigation that might follow, put up notices reading, 'Due to staff changes the Festival Club is temporarily closed' – one way of putting it. There was an enquiry by local health officials. Understandably, Bill did his best to minimize its impact and discourage anyone from attending.

I imagine he thought I might be considering taking the Foundation to court and claiming damages. He was relieved to find this was the last thing on my mind. On the strength of what I imagine he saw as good behaviour, he offered me a job at the School. 'The boys are very young,' he said. 'We need a third member of staff. I think it would be very good to have an older person.' He did not paint a very attractive picture of the work; the salary, he said, was 'derisory' and the hours unsocial. I accepted his offer and embarked on my career at the Britten–Pears School.

John Evans, who later worked for the BBC, first as a music producer and subsequently as Head of Radio 3 Music, and is currently Executive Director and President of the Oregon Bach Festival, had first come to Aldeburgh in 1976 while studying Britten's music for his MA degree. He and a fellow student were working on Britten scores in the Red House Library when Peter Pears unexpectedly came in. John Evans said that he finally plucked up the courage to ask Pears whether Mr Britten would be kind enough to sign their scores. 'I'm sure he will,' Pears replied. 'Just leave them on the kitchen table.' Then to John's surprise Pears said, 'We're having a party in the garden tomorrow. Why don't you both come?' The following day Benjamin Britten's life peerage was announced and the garden party was to celebrate it.

John Evans returned to Aldeburgh as a Hesse student for the 1977 and 1978 Festivals. The Hesse Student Scheme was financed by Princess Margaret of Hesse and the Rhine, who with her husband Prince Ludwig had been a long-standing friend and supporter of Britten and Pears. The scheme funded students, mainly from Britain and Germany, to attend the Festival in return for general assistance such as putting out chairs and peeling potatoes. In 1978 a brief academic course was offered to previous Hesse students – who came to be known as 'super-Hesses' – with a variety of seminars led by Donald Mitchell and William Swinburne.

Following this course John Evans was invited by Donald Mitchell to work with him on his book *Benjamin Britten: Pictures from a Life*. John was no longer in receipt of a grant and he needed regular employment. Diana Servaes, who had

© Nigel Luckhurst

Students, faculty and observers at a 1978 Singers course. Theodor Uppman and Nancy Evans are in the centre, with lutenist Robert Spencer far left, with, behind him and to the right soprano Lynne Dawson, and, behind her and to the right, pianist Roger Vignoles. The front row includes the School's first Administrator for Singers courses, Diana Servaes (far left), and soprano Philippa Dames-Longworth (third from the right). Choir conductor Olive Quantrill is on the far right, with, behind her, Anne Surfling and Pamela Wheeler (partly obscured), who are now archive assistants at the Britten–Pears Library.

I owe my whole career to Aldeburgh and we were all privileged to be there in that special atmosphere that was entirely dedicated to excellence. There was good training elsewhere but Aldeburgh gave us a level to aspire to – it made us all what we are today.

JOHN EVANS

I owe Bill a huge amount, we all do. Anything that seemed sloppy was anathema to Servaes and I remember very clearly how furious he could be if he came across a poster or notice advertising a concert that had already taken place. We were always very careful to go around the town removing posters of the event that had taken place the previous evening.

JOHN OWEN

been administering the courses for Singers, was leaving and it was suggested that Evans should apply for the job: 'I applied, but Bill [Servaes] didn't want me. He thought that I would be a spy for one of the other factions at Aldeburgh.' However, to John's amazement and against all the odds, he did get the job. Servaes's suspicions were typical of the paranoid atmosphere that pervaded the whole organization at the time.

None of us knew exactly what we should be doing – I far less than the other two – but we managed to keep everything going and worked incredibly hard for the first ten weeks of the 1979 courses. The timetable was punishing. The courses that summer were all one week long and were held back to back, starting on a Sunday afternoon with the students arriving at 2 p.m. for a sing- or play-through. The staff members were at the School from about 1 p.m. The sing-through stopped at 6 p.m. on those first Sundays of the course and, after ensuring that the students were returned to Aldeburgh and could be fed, we left the building and started again every day of the week at 9 a.m.

The School's working day during the week ended at about 6 p.m. but there was usually a lecture or seminar on some evenings and consequently for three nights a week the School closed at 10 p.m. On Saturdays there were rehearsals followed by an 8 p.m. concert in Snape Maltings Concert Hall. We were free on Sunday mornings and when at 2 p.m. the new students arrived the whole weekly routine started again; that continued for ten weeks without a break.

I cannot remember ever being so exhausted and neither can the two Directors' Assistants. John Owen developed a constant cough which sounded positively life threatening and John Evans simply got paler and paler until he looked more like a ghost than a human being. Eventually I went to Bill Servaes and said that I was seriously concerned about the health of the 'boys' and that I thought that they should each be given at least one day off work during the ten weeks. 'Well, I'm not in the slightest bit worried,' was Bill's surprising reply. 'Just think what young men of that age were doing during the war and stop fussing.' I went back to the School with my tail between my legs and we all just carried on until the end of the courses.

During that first summer, while John Evans was at his most ghost-like and most stressed, the 'black spaghetti' incident occurred during an Early Music course. It is a perfect illustration of how inexperienced we were and, as everything was run on a shoestring, how ill-equipped. Dr Basil Lam, harpsichordist and early music specialist, was to give a lecture to the students. He told John Evans that he would be bringing with him a particularly precious tape of music examples to illustrate his talk and requested that a tape recorder should be made available.

The School had only fairly basic equipment and John could not find an appropriate machine. Eventually one of the singers lent him a portable 'ghetto-blaster', which was hardly suitable but the best we could do. In the event, just as Basil Lam was about to start his lecture, John, always the perfectionist, decided to make sure that everything was in order and inserted the tape. He switched the machine on; to our horrified gaze it went into what John describes as 'auto-destruct mode' and what looked like black spaghetti started spewing uncontrollably out of the tape recorder. John's face was ashen and as he lent over the machine, I stood behind him, with my arms spread out, in an attempt to prevent Dr Lam from seeing the disaster that was unfolding. The tape was by now everywhere. We grabbed handfuls of the stuff off the floor but, of course, as we did that, more and more of it was still spewing out of the machine; we could only look at each other horrified, speechless and helpless.

Eventually, after what seemed like eternity and after frantically pressing various knobs, John, miraculously it seemed, persuaded the machine to stop spitting out the tape and then to roll it back. Basil Lam never knew how close his lecture came to total disaster and so scarred were we that when John and I met recently to talk about the first year of the School, it was the event that we both remembered most clearly. The only difference is that now it seems funny.

An important beneficial element in creating the benign atmosphere was that the School would not allow any prizes or competitions and as a result there was no competitiveness among the students. 'It wasn't about who was best but about everyone doing their best,' John Evans remembered. 'And this applied not only to the students but to everyone who worked there too.'

© Nigel Luckhurst

A rare moment of calm: John Owen outside the School's office area

John Owen first worked at Aldeburgh in 1978 and in 1979 was appointed Assistant to the Director of String Studies. It is generally agreed that what the School was to become over the next twelve years was to a large extent due to John Owen's total commitment. We all learned from our years at the School but John Owen in particular remembers the powerful influence of Bill Servaes, who was a stickler for correctness and detail in matters of correspondence and presentation.

In 1980 John Evans left the School and went to work as a researcher at the Britten–Pears Library and I became Registrar. John Owen took over as the Administrator of both String and Singers Courses in 1981, continuing in this role until 1991. He was totally in tune with what the School was setting out to achieve and nothing was too much effort for him to enable it to reach that goal. His loyalty and his dedication were unflagging and both teachers and students from all over the world remember with gratitude the extraordinary lengths to which he would go to look after them.

Owen had already helped to structure the auditions for the Snape Maltings Training Orchestra and the String courses; the development of international auditions for the Singers courses was very much his own achievement. However, his greatest contribution depended on his creative imagination. He had an almost instinctive ability to cast singers into the right roles for the Opera courses, to help steer their careers and to suggest artists that he thought would make the most interesting and valuable teachers.

After leaving the School in 1991 John Owen became a successful agent and manager. Today his artists talk about the way he cares for them and for their careers and the trouble he takes over their engagements – qualities developed during his time at the Britten–Pears School.

All the students lived with Aldeburgh landladies and were transported to and from Aldeburgh in the School minibus. While the English bed-and-breakfast set-up was familiar to British students, many of our students came from Europe and North America and to them life with an English landlady was something never before encountered – particularly as the Aldeburgh landladies were such a special breed.

Patricia Mooring (now Lady Maddocks) has a highly developed sense of humour. This was something she certainly needed in her job of arranging all the student accommodation. This was a huge task, rivalling the complexity of hotel booking arrangements, but she seemed to manage to keep both the students and the landladies happy and any near-disasters when bookings mysteriously went wrong were quietly averted and any hint of problems exquisitely covered up.

Bearing in mind that some of the students were volatile characters and that some thought that they were already stars, it is remarkable that there was as little friction as there was, but if any problems did arise it was Patricia Mooring who dealt with them, treating both the student and the landlady even-handedly and restoring peace and calm. Patricia, herself, had students to stay with her. At this time she lived in a very pretty house in Aldeburgh High Street with a small annexe at the back, where the students lived. Melvin Earl-Brown, the black American counter-tenor, loved Patricia Mooring and was a frequent guest of hers. He used to say, 'I'm out at the back in the slaves' quarters.'

For many of the ladies of Aldeburgh having students to stay was heaven sent. Some of them were quite grand but discreetly hard up; often they were long-standing Aldeburgh residents, frequently music-lovers, and this was a way of making a little money and at the same time having the interest of young musicians staying in the house. And they all genuinely wanted to help the School. They provided comfortable accommodation (and enormous breakfasts) and they really looked after their guests, especially students from abroad to whom living in Aldeburgh was an entirely new and rather strange experience.

It was touching to see the landladies attending the masterclasses as observers to see and take a pride in 'their' students. Many lifelong friendships were forged. One of the landladies was Julia Lang, of *Listen with Mother* fame (the originator of the invitation, 'Are you sitting comfortably? Then I'll begin'); she is fondly remembered by many former students. Beth Welford occasionally provided accommodation for students and told someone the story of one particular student saying, 'Of course, I don't really know what I'm doing here, I can't stand Britten's music.' Mrs Welford did not let on that she was, in fact, the composer's sister.

The Aldeburgh landladies tended to be an eccentric breed. While more than willing to provide the 'full English' breakfast, there was often a reluctance to ensure a constant supply of hot water or central heating, which, in their no-nonsense British way, some considered a quite unnecessary luxury. For many of the North American students the unwonted cold is etched on their memories. Summer in Suffolk can be a surprisingly bracing experience and the American and Canadian students were not accustomed to the hardy attitude of the Aldeburgh residents.

Not all aspiring landladies were accepted by Patricia Mooring, who was inflexible in her demands for high standards. She inspected each house and made sure that the accommodation on offer was acceptable. It was she who decided how much should be paid for the students' bed and breakfast. She did the costings in minute detail: so many eggs, so many rashers of bacon, toast, tea and coffee, heating for so many hours and the cost of washing a certain number of towels, sheets and pillowcases. A charge of £12.50 per night was agreed in the first years of the School.

Students were made warmly welcome in the town; they were young, bright and gifted and brought a liveliness to Aldeburgh that had previously been seen only during the Festival or the holiday season. They were welcomed not only for themselves but for the additional income they brought to the landladies and to the few restaurants – and, of course, to the pubs, where groups of them gathered every evening, and to the famous Aldeburgh fish-and-chip shop at the southern end of the High Street, which was a favourite with everybody. The students all worked hard and for long hours, but they did not allow social life (or romance, which could sometimes be quite steamy and dramatic) to suffer as a result. They became a familiar feature of Aldeburgh life in the summer and memorable end-of-course parties were given, sometimes organized by the students themselves and sometimes at the invitation of Aldeburgh residents. Over very many years, Hugo and Margaret Herbert-Jones were always willing to have students in their house and gave wonderful parties in their garden where highly competitive games of croquet were played, parties still happily remembered by former students all over the world.

This relationship between the students and their landladies was very important. If hostel accommodation had been available when the School was starting, something very valuable would certainly have been lost. At Snape the students got to know one another and their teachers and they mingled during the working day with fellow musicians, but by living in the houses of Aldeburgh residents they actually got to know Suffolk people and, as a consequence, their experience of their time at the School was all the richer.

Food for both the students and the teachers at the School was a perpetual problem. The School had been designed with a very small kitchen, with a serving bar in the front, and facilities for making tea and coffee – but not much else. This was before the days of the microwave oven. The students were picked up every morning in Aldeburgh in the minibus driven by Mark Stevens, our original minibus driver, and brought out to Snape, arriving at about 9.30 a.m. Often they were at the School until late in the evening and, although they might have had a generous cooked breakfast, it was very important to provide them with coffee and tea throughout the day, and with a meal of sorts at lunchtime.

The baker in Aldeburgh sold floury, white buns. In an attempt to solve the catering dilemma, I used to collect a supply of these buns in a large thick paper bag before going out to Snape. As a result, I always seemed to have white flour on my clothes and often, I was told, on my face. At the same time we bought supplies of sliced cheese and ham but, sadly, that seemed to be the extent of the available choice. I can't imagine now why we were not able to provide a little more variety. Perhaps we could not afford anything else and so cheese or ham it was.

During that first full summer in our own building, in 1979, Pip Talbot entered our lives and proved to be the perfect person to help with the catering. She was a pretty, blond, rather round, middle-aged and very jolly widow who lived in Aldeburgh and who said that she would be happy to run the kitchen and feed the staff and students. With a permanent smile, every day she would ask, 'Tea or coffee?' 'Ham or cheese?'

Of course, there were always a few grumbles and Artur Balsam, teaching at the School, was once heard to say, 'Unusually, today, we have ham or cheese.' On the whole everyone accepted the difficulties and put up quite cheerfully with the repetitiveness of the menu. Pip loved the students and she enjoyed rubbing shoulders with the celebrated musicians who were teaching at the School. Her smile and bubbly personality are well remembered even now; when I went to Toronto in 2008 to talk to some of the Canadian students, she was one of the people they all remembered.

Evening meals could present even more of a challenge than the ham-or-cheese lunch. During the week the students ate in Aldeburgh, often at the reopened Festival Club, which offered a discounted rate to the students and, if the schedule allowed them to get back in time, there were sufficient pubs and restaurants offering inexpensive meals. But as the first day of the courses always fell on a Sunday there was always the likelihood that there would be nothing open by the time the students got back to Aldeburgh.

We tried various ways to feed them and I finally persuaded the Plough and Sail at Snape to provide a hot evening meal in the School on Sundays but, sadly, this seemingly good idea proved disastrous. We would carefully count the number of students, order the appropriate number of dinners and then have to reduce them as students exercised their right to refuse the meal, often feeling unable to afford what was on offer, or preferring to make their own arrangements.

David Grimwood was in charge of the kitchen at the Plough and Sail. He was a very good chef who went on to become a successful restaurateur. He was normally a charming person

Tchaikovsky: Eugene Onegin
Aldeburgh Festival, 1979

Madame Larina	Marilyn de Blieck
Tatiana	Marie McLaughlin
	Elizabeth Brice
Filipievna	Nuala Willis
Vladimir Lensky	Adrian Thompson
Eugene Onegin	Richard Jackson
Prince Gremin	Ingemar Korjus
Trifon Petrovich	Simon Phipps
Zaretsky	John Hancorn
M. Triquet	Peter Pears
Guillot	Eric Crozier

Snape Maltings Training Orchestra
Leader Malcolm Layfield
Conducted by Mstislav Rostropovich
Directed by Christopher Renshaw
Designed by Robin Don

but he had the sort of temper that we have now become accustomed to seeing in today's TV chefs' programmes. On the last occasion that we tried to provide dinners I had had to reduce the numbers twice, perhaps three times, and eventually he stormed into the School with flashing eyes, swore roundly at me in true Gordon Ramsay style, and then flatly refused to send over any food at all. That was the end of the experiment and we gave up trying to provide student evening meals at the School; this particular catering problem had defeated us and the students just had to make their own plans for dinner on Sundays and every other evening.

In 1979 the actual School courses proper, as became customary, started in July but performances of *Eugene Onegin*, conducted by Mstislav Rostropovich, had been given as part of the June Festival. This very successful project was not strictly part of the School programme but it involved singers who had all studied at Snape and the orchestra was the Snape Maltings Training Orchestra, led by Malcolm Layfield. It was considered a School event in all but name and was certainly the first large-scale project in which the School played such a central part. Hilary Keenlyside was the Concerts Manager of the Aldeburgh Festival and she was responsible for the management of the event.

The producer was Christopher Renshaw and the designer was Robin Don. Don had produced models of the design during the planning stages only to have them rejected, one by one, by Galina Vishnevskaya who, as the course director, was

© Nigel Luckhurst

Eugene Onegin: Marie McLaughlin (Tatiana) and Richard Jackson (Onegin)

© Nigel Luckhurst

Eugene Onegin: The duel – John Hancorn (Zaretsky), Eric Crozier (Guillot) and Richard Jackson (Onegin)

© Nigel Luckhurst

Wolfgang Mehlhorn

very much involved in the production. 'No,' she would say each time yet another model was shown to her. A compromise was finally reached and opera of a very high standard was presented. Peter Pears himself sang the cameo role of M. Triquet.

Courses in that first year were very varied. After *Eugene Onegin* there was a String Quartet course with the Amadeus Quartet teaching and with eight quartets on the course, including the Takács-Nagy Quartet, later known simply as the Takács Quartet. Also on the course was the Brodsky Quartet, who were to become regulars at Snape. The first course scheduled to take place in the new building as a part of the School's year, was a Chamber Music course for wind, strings and piano with Artur Balsam, Thea King, Murray Perahia and Wolfgang Mehlhorn giving masterclasses.

There were places for registered observers on all the courses. They attended the series of masterclasses and came to all the subsidiary events. There were also casual observers who could opt to attend individual classes. These observers, both regular and casual, were a vital feature of the School's programme and provided an informed audience for the classes as well as being a much needed source of revenue. Many of the observers registered for courses throughout the season and became familiar faces to both the students and the staff, entering actively into the life of the School.

One of the most faithful observers was David Heckels, who was the Foundation's solicitor and a member of the Council. He played an important part in all the activities of the Festival

© Nigel Luckhurst

Faculty members for the Chamber Music course: Wolfgang Mehlhorn, Murray Perahia, Nicola Grunberg, Hugh Maguire and Milan Vitek

© Nigel Luckhurst

Murray Perahia with Annette Cole of the Trio Zingara

© Nigel Luckhurst

Artur Balsam

and of the School and was always ready to advise and help in every way that he could. He could often be seen sitting at the back of the Recital Room, observing the masterclasses, adding to his already extensive musical knowledge. David Heckels was a valued member of the Aldeburgh family and his advice on a variety of matters of importance was constantly sought and always valued. Everyone knew that behind his self-effacing manner there was a shrewd brain and that his advice would always be thoughtful and fair – and given in the context of his unswerving loyalty to the Foundation and all that it represented. Later he was to become Chairman of the Aldeburgh Foundation.

Among the students participating on the Chamber Music course were the Trio Zingara, which comprised three rather glamorous girls. I remember how worried the violinist, Anni Schnarch, was when she was required to return to Israel to do her military service. The risk of her hands being injured caused her profound anxiety.

Artur Balsam was then an elderly man of great charm with a wonderfully dry sense of humour. Very dapper, he always came to the classes dressed formally in a three-piece suit. A Polish-born American, after the rise of Nazism he had fled to the United States where he taught at the Manhattan School of Music. Renowned as a prize-winning pianist, particularly in the world of chamber music, he had been one of Murray Perahia's teachers in New York and it was at Perahia's invitation that he came to the School. He inspired the students as both a

© Nigel Luckhurst

Wolfgang Mehlhorn with the Liadov Quartet

© Nigel Luckhurst

Thea King directs a wind ensemble

1979

Singers Courses

The Faculty included:
Janet Craxton   Nancy Evans
Daniel Ferro   Peter Pears
Robert Spencer

Students included:
Marilyn de Blieck, Philippa Dames-Longworth, Lynne Dawson, Alasdair Elliott, John Hancorn, Gareth Morrell, Catherine Robbin, Brian Scott
from the USA:
Stanley Cornett, Melvin Earl-Brown, Robert Puleo, Douglas Robinson, Joseph Tambornino, Andrew Yarosh

String Courses

The Faculty included:
Felix Andrievsky   Karoly Botvay
Csaba Erdélyi   Hugh Maguire
William Pleeth   Jacqueline du Pré

© Nigel Luckhurst

Robert Spencer with Philippa Dames-Longworth

remarkable performer and an equally remarkable teacher. They knew how fortunate they were to have the benefit of his vast experience.

Peter Pears was Director of Singing Studies and Nancy Evans his co-Director. Pears had great gifts as a teacher and talking now to his former students, the overwhelming impression is one of gratitude for having been given the opportunity to study with this legendary singer. He was always very gentle with the singers and gave them his fullest attention, but when one of them did not quite measure up to his expectations, he was apt to say, 'Very nice, my dear. What else have you got?'

Pears was always astonishingly modest. Talking one day about his own voice he said to John Evans, 'I think I have made the best of what I have been given.' Evans remembers Pears telling him of a visit to the Royal Opera House to hear Margaret Price and Plácido Domingo in *Otello*. He said afterwards, 'I have been given a singing lesson by Plácido.'

Nancy Evans undertook the private consultations. She would listen to the students in the first sing-through, taking copious notes, and then each student would have a consultation with her in which she would try to identify any vocal problems. She showed great sensitivity; she was always very conscious of the fact that they all had other teachers in the conservatoires where they were studying and she was at great pains to be certain not to create further problems that might unfold when they returned to their regular teachers.

© Nigel Luckhurst

An unidentified lutenist with soprano Lynne Dawson and Peter Pears

I remember my times at the Britten–Pears School with enormous affection; I loved the atmosphere and the surroundings and of course the quality of the teaching was wonderful. I met musicians who were subsequently hugely important to me – Peter [Pears], of course, an inspirational, and exacting, teacher; Robert Spencer, Rae Woodland, Anthony Rolfe Johnson, Graham Johnson, and so on. I did not have the opportunity of an undergraduate (or postgraduate) programme and so my times at the School were of especial benefit to me.

LYNNE DAWSON

© Nigel Luckhurst

Peter Pears and Daniel Ferro with a student

Among the students for the Early Music course were Lynne Dawson, now Head of Vocal Studies at the Royal Northern, and Paul Ekins. It was the first course to be attended by Jane Leslie Mackenzie, a protégée of the Canadian Aldeburgh Foundation.

In the early years courses were arranged with singers working alongside instrumentalists. The Schütz and Bach course had oboist Janet Craxton supervising the instrumentalists and Daniel Ferro and Peter Pears the singers. Schubert, Schumann and English Song courses were to follow.

Philippa ('Pippa') Dames-Longworth was a regular student at the School between 1977 and 1979 and was a great favourite of Peter Pears, who became a real friend of hers. He loved her voice and did everything he could to encourage her career. She says that she adored Peter and can never be grateful enough for all the help he gave her. She tells the story of singing Britten's 'On this Island' from the early song-cycle of the same name for Peter in a masterclass and feeling very nervous and vulnerable about her interpretation into which she had put a great deal of thought. Her heart sank when she finished and there was, for a moment, complete silence. Then Peter said, 'Well, my dear, I've never heard it sung *quite* like that before.' This was followed by yet another silence during which Pippa steeled herself to hear the worst and then Peter said with a smile, 'But I think Ben would have loved it.'

Pippa Longworth continued to have a successful career, which suffered for a while after she struck a severe vocal problem; happily, this is now resolved and her career is back on track. In fact, the majority of the students on the 1979 courses went on to achieve success.

In August, after the Schubert and Schumann course, there were masterclasses for solo strings. Hugh Maguire was now the Director of String Studies and he invited Jacqueline du Pré, who was an old friend, to come to Snape to give a class.

Although she was by this time seriously ill, and in a wheelchair, she was still able to teach and inspire the young players. She was accompanied to Snape by her husband Daniel Barenboim and a nurse. As the school dogsbody it fell to me to arrange her meals. My instructions were very precise: steamed fish and boiled potatoes with absolutely no flavouring, not even salt. I remember taking her horrid-looking lunch to her and feeling so sad that not only did she have a dreadful illness to cope with but that she also had to live on such unappetizing fare.

One of the students attending this masterclass was Ofra Harnoy, the daughter of Israeli parents who had made their home in Canada. Hugh Maguire, while recognizing her exceptional talent, was initially uncertain about accepting her as she was so very young. In the event he decided to let her attend and her parents came with her, her mother accompanying her for the classes. Daniel Barenboim was sitting in the Recital Room listening to the class with Hugh Maguire. Hugh turned to him and said, 'What are we going to do with this child?' 'Well, shoot the mother first' was the response from someone sitting near by who had overheard the question.

Jacqueline du Pré working with cellist Torlief Thedeen

Britten: The Rape of Lucretia
Workshop performances 1979

Male Chorus	Alasdair Elliott
	Gordon Christie
	Stanley Cornett
	Douglas Robinson
Female Chorus	Andrea Baron
Lucretia	Susan Smith-Tyrell
Lucretia/Bianca	Marilyn de Blieck
	Catherine Robbin
Lucia	Dorothy Eschweiller
	Delith Brook
	Joy Puritz
Bianca	Carol Ann Leatherby
	Janice Greaves
	Yolande Jones
Tarquinius	Paul Ekins
	John Fox
Junius	John Hancorn
Collatinus	Michael Neill

Snape Maltings Training Orchestra
Conducted by David Parry
Directed by Eric Crozier

Following the success of the first Britten Symposium in February 1978, held in the Festival Gallery (now the Peter Pears Gallery) in Aldeburgh, there were two academic weekend courses in 1979, a Composition course with Harrison Birtwistle and John Casken lecturing, and a Wagner Study weekend with Donald Mitchell, Patrick Carnegy, Arnold Whittall, Philip Winters and Frederika Wagner.

Elizabeth Melville, the wife of Sir Eugene Melville, who was the Chairman of the Aldeburgh Festival–Snape Maltings Foundation, was a participant on the Wagner course. She had a great interest in music and, after she was widowed and well into her eighties, developed a love of contemporary music. She would travel alone to attend the Huddersfield Contemporary Music Festival each year. As Chairman, her husband, Sir Eugene, had been such a stalwart supporter of the School and Elizabeth continued for the rest of her life to take a lively interest in all its activities, giving it her fullest support.

In September the School held a two-week opera workshop on Britten's *The Rape of Lucretia*, leading to two performances in the Maltings, with Eric Crozier as director and David Parry conducting. Crozier had directed the first production of the opera at Glyndebourne in 1946 and had a special understanding of its subtleties.

Crozier had worked closely with Britten and Pears in the early days of the English Opera Group. As had happened with a number of Britten's colleagues and collaborators over the years, there had been a break in the friendship. Peter Pears's tremendous affection for Nancy Evans, Crozier's wife, was unwavering and, with Nancy undertaking a major role at the School, Crozier was reinstated to the Aldeburgh circle.

Although there was some adverse criticism of his production of *The Rape of Lucretia*, on the whole it was very successful and many who saw it still remember with pleasure the scene of the Folding of the Linen. It was a testimony to Eric's imagination and aesthetic sense.

The School's year ended in November when it provided the venue for the Ensemble Singers course. For the School staff this course entailed a huge amount of work. Dealing with a large number of amateur singers was always fraught with difficulties; generally speaking they were far more demanding than our usual run of students. I regret to say we developed a collective prejudice against the course and came to dread it. Among ourselves it was known irreverently as the 'Knit Your Own Violin' course.

However, Peter Pears loved it and entered enthusiastically and wholeheartedly into its spirit and insisted that we hold it every year. On the 1979 course there were fifty singers, women far outnumbering men, in four choirs. A few of those who attended have gone on to professional careers but the vast majority remained amateurs.

Burned into the memory is one all-female choir who had designed their own costumes – uniforms might be a better description – which were bright pink, shiny and tight-fitting, and did little to enhance the appearance.

Of course, Pears was right. The participants adored him and valued every moment of their time, singing their hearts out and no doubt taking away very valuable experiences and lessons.

The members of staff were very relieved when the first full season came to an end. We were pleased and perhaps slightly surprised, that, on the whole, it had gone so well. We were all too tired to celebrate and John Evans says now that all he can really remember of the whole of that first year is the feeling of utter exhaustion. The fact was that it had been a success; I think that we had a very clear vision of what had been achieved and, more importantly, what could be achieved in the future.

The year 1980 brought changes to the School staff. John Evans left to take up his research post at the Britten–Pears Library. Donald Mitchell asked me to take on the role of Registrar, which sounds much grander than it was, and in the 1980 Aldeburgh Festival Programme Book John Owen, Jessica Ford and Virginia Caldwell are listed as assistants.

John Owen continued to administer the String courses, displaying his talent for administration and his instinct for programming. Hugh Maguire selected all the players for the String courses but Owen worked very closely with him to ensure that only the most suitable students were selected.

Jessica Ford was in charge of the Singers courses and Virginia Caldwell was the School's Secretary.

As a member of the staff, I was able to sit in on at least part of every class. This was a job bonus beyond my dreams. By it my own (amateur) musical education was immeasurably enhanced. The Singers courses, in particular, took me to a new appreciation of vocal performance across the broadest possible repertoire. This was, and still must be, the experience of the hundreds of observers who, over the years, paid small sums to sit in on masterclasses at Snape. End-of-course recitals were memorable because one could recall the moments during the previous week's classes when a student had broken through what had seemed an impossible technical barrier. A string ensemble would perform a subtle pianissimo passage that had seemed unachievable during their coaching sessions, or repertoire that had appeared far too ambitious in the first day's run-through was performed with great polish.

VIRGINIA CALDWELL

During the 1979 season, despite our exhaustion and the steepness of the learning curve, the atmosphere had generally been a happy one. In 1980 this changed and there was considerable tension throughout the year. The School flourished and continued to develop but the staffing structure produced a new raft of problems.

Looking back, I think that the main difficulty was that the roles we undertook had not been clearly defined and certainly had not been well thought through. Apart from this, the School staff always had to tread a somewhat difficult path; we were answerable to the General Manager, to the School Directors and to Donald Mitchell, who chaired the Education Committee.

Bill Servaes was still the General Manager and was entirely supportive of the School staff but he had his own problems with the overall administration. As far as the actual running of the School was concerned, we were largely left to our own devices. Peter Pears and Hugh Maguire, as the Directors of Singing Studies and String Studies, were the final authority on all artistic matters; they were an unfailing help and support to the staff, showing great understanding of all the difficulties that we met – but not all our masters shared that attitude. However, despite these problems and tensions, there was such a degree of good will and determination on everyone's part to see the School succeed that these difficulties were generally resolved. John Owen and I had the experience of one season behind us, but, nevertheless, it remained all very new and we were still learning.

The artistic programme of the School, its *raison d'être*, overseen by Pears and Maguire, was, of course, fundamental to every decision; in order for it all to run smoothly there were a lot of elements to be borne in mind if the experience of faculty and students at Snape was to be happy and productive. The scheduling of classes and private coaching had to be both fair and efficient. Catering and accommodation were also vital to the general welfare of the students and faculty if they were to get the maximum benefit from their time at Snape. It should be remembered, too, that we were always working on an extremely limited budget, where every penny counted, and apart from the daily routine, we had to deal with publicity and brochures, fees and bursaries, transport schedules – as well as the fragile egos of many of the participants.

Jessica Ford, the daughter of Professor Boris Ford, who had been involved with the early beginnings of the School, had been an orchestral cellist and had chosen to switch to a career in arts administration. In 1981 she decided to move on and subsequently became the wife of Roger Vignoles. She went on to success as an artists' agent in London. Virginia Caldwell, an American, had been working for Radio Orwell, an independent radio station based in Ipswich and was to have a long and substantial career at Aldeburgh, first with the School from 1980 to 1982, eventually running the Friends organization for the Aldeburgh Foundation very successfully. She was a benign influence in the School and was a popular member of staff.

John Owen and Hugh Maguire

Haim Taub of the Tel Aviv Quartet guiding a student ensemble during the Fourth International Academy of String Quartets

In April 1980 the Fourth Academy of String Quartets took place under the direction of the Tel Aviv Quartet. Quartets studying on the course included the Endellion, the Fairfield, the Guadagnini, the Rawe, the Howard and the Alexandra. The quiet, rural atmosphere of Snape was a far cry from Tel Aviv and suddenly the School was transformed by the four larger-than-life Israelis whose warmth and ebullience made an indelible impression, not only on the students, but on the staff and on everyone who observed the classes. Daniel Benyamini was the principal viola of the Israel Philharmonic Orchestra, a position he was to hold for thirty years. He was also the Chairman of the Orchestra and a very important figure in Israeli music. The first violin, Haim Taub and the cellist, Uzi Wiesel, both members of the IPO, were popular with the students. With such distinguished musicians teaching and with such talented quartets participating, this course achieved magnificently the aims of the School.

Between July and September the Singers courses included a French Song Course and an English Song course with John Shirley-Quirk teaching. In September the School held a two-week course on Britten's *Albert Herring* with Eric Crozier, the opera's librettist, directing.

There were students from Canada and the United States in the cast including Henry Ingram, the Canadian who played the Vicar and whose impressions of Snape were quoted on p. 16. There were two performances in the Maltings and the course was considered a success. I suppose that one thing that the members of staff remember most vividly was Eric's extraordinary demand that Nancy Evans should be considered a stage hand and wear an SMTO sweat shirt, the backstage uniform, at all the performances. Astonishingly, she agreed to this eccentricity with remarkable grace and a great deal of laughter.

During the first weekend of this course the Mayor of Aldeburgh was installed; this involved a procession from the Parish Church down the hill to the Moot Hall for the actual ceremony. The Mayor in 1980 was Elizabeth Roney and she was required to wear robes, the mayoral chain and a large official hat festooned with feathers round the brim. The Canadian and American students on the *Albert Herring* course stood open-mouthed on the pavement outside the Church, watching the procession in utter disbelief. It really was *Albert Herring* come to life. Among the students attending the Singers courses in 1980 was Joy Puritz, the granddaughter of Elisabeth Schumann.

There were two SMTO courses in 1980. The first was conducted by Alexander Schneider and all the players gained immeasurably from working under his direction. The orchestra list included not only Douglas Boyd (see also p. 72), but many others who are all now well-known figures in the music profession (see p. 119). The second course was conducted by Hugh Maguire with Nobuko Imai as the soloist.

In August a course for Solo String Players was held with William Pleeth and Wolfgang Marschler teaching; the students came from as far afield as Brazil and Japan as well as from North America and various European countries. The students

© *Nigel Luckhurst*

Nancy Evans and Eric Crozier rehearsing *Albert Herring*

© Nigel Luckhurst

Artur Balsam working with students during the 1980 Trios course

included Ofra Harnoy, Bernhard Biberauer and Rhydian Shaxson. This was followed by the First International Academy of String Trios. Among the trios on the course were the Trio Zingara and the Hunt Trio from Dublin: Fionnuala, Una and Vincent, a brother and two sisters. Una Hunt has had a successful career as a pianist and musicologist and Fionnuala was at one time the Artistic and Music Director of the Irish Chamber Orchestra. She has had a very successful solo career and is now one of the leaders of the World Orchestra for Peace.

Also in 1980, Donald Mitchell introduced Thai music and Thai musicians to the School. Interest in ethnomusicology is now quite common but it was then a ground-breaking development when these exotic musicians from Bangkok arrived at the School. Interest in their music and their instruments was high and there were students from all over the country anxious to take advantage of such an unusual opportunity. Donald Mitchell lectured and recounted his experiences of music in Thailand. There is no doubt that this visit made an important contribution to the growing reputation of the School and the variety of its programme. Donald Mitchell told me that he thought that it was a very significant development in the study of music in Britain.

The Thai Ensemble was made up of musicians to the Royal Court in Thailand who brought their instruments and costumes to Snape. Their first concert was held in the Recital Room and the first three or four rows of the raked seating had to be kept empty as the musicians felt that otherwise they

I first attended the Britten–Pears School in the summer of 1980. I was studying in Vienna at the time and I still clearly recollect the hugely positive influence the courses had on my playing. So much so that I returned for three subsequent summers. I took a variety of courses – some chamber music and some solo.

Outstanding teachers were the order of the day at the Britten–Pears and the ones who really stood out for me were Josef Gingold and the members of the Beaux Arts Trio. Hugh Maguire was Director of String Studies and he had the great gift of identifying the best and most suitable teachers, and then recruiting them for the school. Hugh is a charismatic man and it was thanks to the strength of his personality that the school was such a vibrant and rewarding institution, for students and teachers alike.

It wasn't all work either. We frequently repaired to the aptly named 'Potty' Bar, from whose ceiling dangled an enticing array of said receptacles . . .

FIONNUALA HUNT

© *Amelia Stein*

Fionnuala Hunt

would be too close to the feet of the audience. Dacre Raikes, a member of a distinguished English family, lived in Bangkok and was the Adviser and Administrator to the Classical Dance and Music Groups of Srinakharinwirot University. He travelled with the musicians. No one there will ever forget the astonishing sight of Donald Mitchell and Dacre Raikes performing the Horse Dance in the Recital Room at the end of the concert.

Extraordinarily, the Thai musicians also took part in a procession along the High Street in Aldeburgh. It was certainly very strange to see these Thai men, in their exotic costumes, playing their instruments and walking among the solid Aldeburgh burghers on a cold and very wet Saturday morning. Nothing quite like it had ever been seen before and the townspeople, who were becoming accustomed to unusual events originating at Snape, were, nevertheless, utterly bemused by the whole experience.

The Thai musicians visited Snape twice and interest in their work continued to be high. Very generously, when they left after their final visit, they donated their instruments to the School and these were stored in an upstairs cupboard at the School. Unfortunately, the instruments were infested with worm and when Bob Ling, the caretaker, discovered this, he told me in no uncertain terms that if I didn't get rid of them, he would burn them. We were all aghast. It was my unhappy task to telephone Donald Mitchell and tell him the news; he very speedily agreed to come and fetch them. Their final fate remains a mystery.

The academic courses in 1980 were a Vaughan Williams Symposium directed by Michael Kennedy, with Ursula Vaughan Williams acting as consultant, and a Lutosławski Symposium in November with the composer conducting the SMTO. This was an incredibly important event in the history of the School. Witold Lutosławski was one of the major European composers of the twentieth century and to have him present at the School, lecturing and mixing informally with the students, was an enormous honour. This was the final course of the year and ended on a high note.

On 1 December Peter Pears suffered a stroke, which left him with reduced movement in his left arm and leg. With great courage and determination he battled to overcome its effects and was quite soon able to walk again with the help of a stick, but he did not ever regain the use of his arm. He taught again in 1981. All the students of that year will recall the problems he had with walking and remember, too, his heroic, unflagging and cheerful commitment to his work at the School.

At the time he wrote to Graham Johnson, ' I must remind myself continually that our beautiful and model School is where I should mostly employ myself in future, and be satisfied with Suffolk.'

The year 1981 saw further changes in the structure of the School and the management of the Aldeburgh Festival–Snape Maltings Foundation. Jessica Ford left Snape and John Owen was appointed the Course Administrator, with overall

Witold Lutosławski rehearsing the Snape Maltings Training Orchestra

1980
Singers Courses

Students included:
Anthony Attwell, Lynne Dawson, Jane Leslie MacKenzie, Hugh Mackey, James McLean, James Morgan, Gareth Morrell, Brian Parsons, Elizabeth Proday, Robert Puleo, Joy Puritz, Christopher Robson, Joan Rodgers, Brian Scott

1980
Snape Maltings Training Orchestra

The Faculty included:
Nobuko Imai
Hugh Maguire
Alexander Schneider

Students included:
Brian Brooks leader
Douglas Boyd, William Conway, Richard Hosford, Ursula Leveaux, Robin O'Neill, Sally-Jane Pendlebury, Andrew Roberts, Nigel Thomas

My time as student and official accompanist on the Britten–Pears School courses was crucially important for me. Arriving at Snape for the first time from London when I was about twenty-one, I was overwhelmed by the magical setting of the School on those exquisite marshes. Looking out over the reeds I simply couldn't believe what a beautiful and atmospheric place this was. Returning over following years to play for the courses of such great artists as Peter Pears and Hugues Cuénod just at the start of my career was an experience I shall never forget. Later Cuénod asked me to play for his debut recital at the Wigmore Hall – a debut at the age of eighty-five!

I usually stayed with one or other of the wonderfully eccentric Aldeburgh landladies and I remember them with tremendous affection. On one memorable occasion a friend lent me a house which was empty. I arrived late at night and was told that I did not need a key as the back door was never locked. Tentatively, in the dark, I located the back door, let myself in and then went to the car to collect my luggage. When I returned I was met by a pale and trembling, terrified man standing at the top of the stairs and asking me in a hoarse whisper what on earth I thought I was doing. I was as shocked as he was and realized that I had let myself into the house next door. I made my excuses and left!

JULIUS DRAKE

responsibility for all the courses; Susan Wilson was appointed his assistant. Virginia Caldwell remained the School Secretary.

At the Aldeburgh Festival–Snape Maltings Foundation, Bill Servaes resigned as General Manager and Jack Phipps was appointed in his place. Phipps's wife Sue was Pears's niece. Phipps had had a long career in arts administration, including a very successful period as the Head of Touring at the Arts Council. He was an ebullient character with fresh, innovative ideas – it was he who originated the Snape Maltings Proms in 1982 – but he was unable to remedy the rather precarious financial situation in which the Foundation found itself.

Jack Phipps's management style was a very different from that of his predecessor. Although the School came under his authority, the pattern of the School year was now well established, and we were all confident of our roles. The change of General Manager made very little difference to the running of the School, especially as Peter Pears, despite his physical limitations, and Hugh Maguire were there to take all the artistic decisions.

What did change was the way we worked after John Owen's appointment as Course Administrator. There is no doubt that even at this early stage he set a seal on the way the School would develop. His uncompromising pursuit of the very highest standards, his dedication to the task in hand and his sensitive and imaginative skills all now came into their own.

The 1981 programme of courses ran pretty well back to back from March until September. It was an ambitious year and started with a four-day Purcell Symposium directed by Wilfrid Mellers, Peter Aston and Paul Esswood. The course was a mixture of the practical and the academic and there were singers, instrumentalists and academic students on the course. There were ten singers, four instrumentalists and thirteen academic students.

Five days after the Purcell Symposium, there was a Britten Symposium directed by Donald Mitchell, Anthony Milner and Geoffrey Shaw with thirty students in attendance. Although these numbers were manageable, the School really worked more effectively with a smaller number of students. The facilities of the building, including the cafeteria, were designed for comparatively low numbers and when we had thirty students plus observers, faculty and the staff, the building was noticeably overcrowded.

On 29 March masterclasses on Twentieth-Century Violin and Viola Concertos began. William Primrose, the US-based viola player, gave a series of masterclasses. Hugh Maguire took the Violin masterclasses. Pianists Peggy Gray and Nicola Grunberg (the widow of Cecil Aronowitz) were the official accompanists.

The students came from all over the world and included Primrose's protégé Jun Takahira who was to became a Principal of the Tokyo Philharmonic Orchestra. William Primrose's classes were unforgettable and it was a great sadness that, due to his ill-health, he was unable to fulfil his promise to return to the School in 1982.

© Nigel Luckhurst

William Primrose giving a masterclass

© Nigel Luckhurst

Gennadi Rozhdestvensky conducting the Snape Maltings Training Orchestra

The day after the end of this Solo String course the Fifth Academy of String Quartets began with the Janáček Quartet teaching and six quartets participating, including the Alexandra, the Colorado and the Hanson Quartets. At this time, of course, Czechoslavakia was behind the Iron Curtain and it was something of a coup to get this Czech quartet to teach at Snape. They were warm and friendly but one was very conscious of the fact that they came from a world very different from the peaceful, relaxed atmosphere of East Suffolk.

At the end of April a Voice and Piano Duos course took place with Peter Pears, Nancy Evans and Roger Vignoles teaching. Among the pianists were Nancy Cooley, Julius Drake (who were both to become official accompanists at the School) and the multi-talented Jeremy Sams whose subsequent career has included writing, translating, conducting, musical direction and composing film music.

I remember that for some unfathomable reason I was required to go with Roger Vignoles to the auditions in a freezing cold room at the Royal College of Music. Some of the aspiring duos were distinctly odd and certainly did not reach the required standard, but Roger was unfailingly kind and gentle with them. In the event, there were ten duos accepted on the course.

Rae Woodland and Morag Noble were coaches on many of the Singers courses dating from the late 1970s and Sue Phipps had, from the very beginning, offered classes in t'ai chi. These were usually held in the afternoons in the Seminar Room and were popular with the students who found the exercises in the form of smoothly flowing movement extremely helpful.

Following the Voice and Piano Duos there was another new departure with the School offering a Film Music course. Directed by Richard Rodney Bennett, Elmer Bernstein, Donald Mitchell and Christopher Palmer, this was another landmark in the story of the School. Elmer Bernstein, who died in 2004, had composed the music for an astonishing two hundred-odd major films and television series, including the scores for *The Magnificent Seven* and *The Great Escape*. His was a household name in the world of film music and it was a testament to the reputation of the School that he agreed to spend a week teaching at Snape. The course ended with a performance of film music by the SMTO in the Maltings with Elmer Bernstein memorably conducting the music from *The Magnificent Seven*.

It was during this course that Cynthia Millar, who was at the time working in the Aldeburgh Festival office, met Elmer Bernstein and as a consequence her life was utterly changed. He introduced Cynthia to the idea that she might study the Ondes Martenot and was subsequently so impressed with her mastery of the instrument that he composed music for her to perform. She became one of the foremost players of the Ondes Martenot, now in demand with orchestras all over the world.

During the Festival of that year Gennadi Rozhdestvensky conducted the SMTO; included in the programme was the Brahms Double Concerto with Michael Thomas playing the violin, and his sister Jackie the cello. They were members of the Brodsky Quartet, which over the years was very much involved with the School and with the Aldeburgh Festival. Brian Brooks led the orchestra. Also scheduled in this Festival was a concert by the Cambridge University Musical Society, conducted by Philip Ledger and with soloists Marilyn de Blieck, Neil Mackie and John Hancorn, all of whom had studied at Snape.

Marilyn de Blieck had attended masterclasses at Snape and sung in *Eugene Onegin*. John Hancorn, who after an illustrious singing career has established a firm reputation as a choral director, was a participant on many of the courses at this period.

In July a Bach course took place with Peter Pears, Nancy Evans, John Carol Case and Hugh Maguire directing. Graham Barber, Ivor Bolton and Stephen Westrop were the harpsichordists. Melvin Earl-Brown and Douglas Robinson returned for this course and Helen Charnock and Marilyn Dale were both students. This was followed by a Schubert course with Peter Pears, Nancy Evans, Gerhard Hüsch and Graham Johnson. Stephen Ralls and Bruce Ubukata, with Anthony Saunders, were the accompanists. This was the famous course when Hüsch and Peter disagreed on so much and Hüsch reduced singers to tears and tantrums and even provoked an outburst of temper from Stephen Ralls who was famously completely unflappable. Michael Stefan, who founded the singing group Cantabile, was also a student on this course.

The English Song and the Spanish and South American Song courses followed. On the English Song course Peter Pears

© Nigel Luckhurst

Pierre Fournier with Lionel Handy

and Nancy Evans were joined by John Shirley-Quirk and lutenist Robert Spencer; Richard Balcombe, Stephen Ralls and Bruce Ubukata were the accompanists. Lynne Dawson, who had attended many courses and who was a regular student at the School was on this course, as also was Gabriella Fontana.

Laura Sarti and Frederick Fuller directed the Spanish and South American Song courses with Ralls, Ubukata and David Mason as accompanists. This course in many ways was almost as difficult as the Hüsch course; Frederick Fuller proved to be very demanding and intransigent, creating considerable challenges for the School staff.

After these Singers courses the String courses started with a Solo Strings course directed by Pierre Fournier, Josef Gingold and Hugh Maguire, with accompanists Peggy Gray and Nicola Grunberg. It was a triumph for the School to attract Pierre Fournier and Josef Gingold to Snape and there was a rush of applicants wanting to study with them. Fournier was, of course, world famous; dubbed the 'aristocrat of cellists', he numbered Julian Lloyd Webber among his pupils. Students on the course were Brian Brooks, Ofra Harnoy, Fionnuala Hunt, Peter Manning and Kari-Lise Ravnan. Russian-born Gingold was at this time considered to be one of the most influential violin teachers in the USA; he taught for thirty years at Indiana University. I remember sitting with him in the porch of the School and him saying to me, 'I have a marvellous student back in the United States. He is only fourteen but do keep a look out for him – his name is Joshua Bell.'

There is no doubt in my mind that the time I spent at the Britten–Pears School gave me the foundation for everything I do today.

The unique feel of Aldeburgh and Snape has been a recurring theme throughout my life. My first experience there was with my youth orchestra, the Redbridge Youth Orchestra. We stayed at the White Lion Hotel! Imagine that these days: I can't afford to stay there as an adult. When my teacher at the Royal Academy of Music, Hugh Maguire, suggested I attended a course at the School it was already somewhere I knew in my bones. I think my first course at the BPS was a Piano Trio course with the Beaux Arts Trio. What struck me immediately was the intimacy of the place, the friendliness and the beautiful feel of the Recital Room where we took turns to perform and learn in front of our fellow young musicians. I made friends for life on these courses, in particular Rachel Maguire, Hugh's daughter, who played in a trio with Julius Drake and myself, and with Robert Lockhart, a brilliant maverick pianist.

Among the highlights that I most remember are a coffee conversation with Lutosławski and playing the Mendelssohn Octet in the Maltings with Hugh and Rostropovich who had us on the edge of our seats when he got lost in the last movement!

I absolutely loved the Bach course and dream of reinstating it. A small chamber group, string quartet and wind, would accompany singers in the cantatas they came to study with great teachers such as Elly Ameling and Peter Pears. It was such a privilege and I learned so much about phrasing and line from the vocal coaching. Peter would (in his later years) just come and sit quietly at the back and his presence was enormous. Nicholas Daniel was the oboist and sometimes Marios Argiros – both are dear friends who I play with regularly today.

I am so grateful for all the riches I imbibed and it made it completely natural for me to become a chamber musician. It was there I learned the language. Lifelong friendships were formed at the School because we were all connected in this beautiful, nurturing environment. It was like being in a special bubble – like eating the most delicious meal, one that you never want to end.

I have many cherished memories of the Britten–Pears Orchestra, which I led for a while. A performance of the Matthew Passion stands out, as does working with Murray Perahia. To be able to play with him as a violinist in my early twenties was, of course, wonderful. He was a great supporter of a chamber group we formed: Serenata. We used to go to his house in Ealing and he would listen and comment and help. We were in heaven.

Hugh Maguire was always an essential ingredient on any instrumental course. His beaming face and naughtiness and love of all things good in music were utterly infectious.

I met my quartet, the Brindisi, on a course at Snape. We were then all in different quartets but we went on to play together for fifteen years and those years gave me some of the

Jacqueline Shave

most meaningful moments of my life. We had the opportunity to study with the great international quartets at Snape. There is nothing better than working incredibly hard on a masterpiece because every part of you wants to do it well. Then the lunch break and walking out among the reeds and feeling the big sky.

I have many other happy memories – such as sinking a few pints in the 'Potty' Bar and then lying on the beach talking incoherently and passionately about music . . . or kissing someone and then creeping back to guesthouses in the early hours . . . It was an awakening in every sense. We would often go back to John Owen's house for a late-night film. He was so great and put up with a lot from us.

When I come back to play at the Festival my soul sings as I make the pilgrimage. I love it so much.

Jacqueline Shave

Peter Manning is now a well-known conductor and became concertmaster of the Royal Opera House. He founded the Britten Quartet in 1986 and is Conductor and Artistic Director of Musica Vitae, Sweden, and the Manning Camerata.

The Solo Strings course was followed by a Piano Trios course with the Beaux Arts Trio: Menahem Pressler, Isidore Cohen and Bernhard Greenhouse. Also giving masterclasses were William Pleeth and Lamar Crowson, who was American but at that time teaching at the College of Music in Rondebosch, Cape Town. There were ten trios studying on this course and there was a remarkable end-of-course concert with a performance by the Beaux Arts Trio.

Singers courses returned with a Schumann and Brahms course, Russian Song and a Wolf course. Gerhard Hüsch was back for the Schumann and Brahms and Galina Vishnevskaya gave some of her most memorable classes during the Russian Song course. Elisabeth Schwarzkopf directed the Wolf course. Students on these courses included Jane Leslie MacKenzie, Hugh Mackey, Brian Robertson, Joan Rodgers and Brian Scott.

The future career of Joan Rodgers as a great British singer was easy to predict. She was a favourite student, not only because of her obvious talent but because she was so well liked by the faculty and by her fellow students, as well as by the School staff. Joan had read Russian at university and found her classes with Vishnevskaya especially productive; in fact, she was later to give two recitals in Moscow and said, 'Singing Russian songs in Russian to a Russian audience was just heaven.' On the

The members of the Beaux Arts Trio – Menahem Pressler, Isidore Cohen and Bernard Greenhouse – direct a student piano trio from the audience.

It struck me recently while looking at an image taken at the Maltings during the Henze Symposium back in the 1980s that the Britten–Pears School was then, as it is now, full of the spirit for which it was created.

I first came across this important source of musical and arts energy and exploration when Cecil Aronowitz brought me down from the North of England as a young student to be a part of a world and musical vision of which I really had little knowledge.

The utter joy of knowing that Benjamin Britten was indeed present, still working and that from time to time his nurse would bring him to our rehearsals was everything that an arts- and music-life-hungry student could have wished for.

The fascination of having a creator so close drove all thoughts of the wonder of music; indeed, the ambience of Snape, the physical geography of Suffolk and its seascape has always accompanied me as a source of great inspiration. The energy of the landscape both in a magical and real sense allows for meaningful work and discovery for so many musicians, and it really was that spirit of discovery that drove me on from that time.

It is the case that both the geographic and musical landscape as envisioned and translated by both Britten and Pears has stayed with me. This has truly been one of my life's great privileges. The knowledge that George Crabbe, E. M. Forster, and W. H. Auden, among Rimbaud, Rilke, Shakespeare and indeed Wilfred Owen, and so much of all our English verse, was used not only as source material but actually reworked, led naturally to a concentrated feeling of an arts hotspot and above all there were questions of serious study, process and the formation of a method of work, which I think we all felt drew back to the intensity and sensibility of creation at the Red House.

The meticulous balance of study and practical music-making which described both Peter Pears and Britten was very much a 'call sign' and somehow stayed all around those searching for that form of inspiration and it certainly allowed for significant development in many wonderful ways for us all.

I, of course, subsequently formed the Britten Quartet, in addition to all my other activities, after gaining permission to use the name from Peter Pears and in that way fully engaged with an international career, driven by chamber music, conducting and music directorships which endure to this day and my musical activities owe an immense debt of gratitude to the well-spring of those early formative years at the Britten–Pears school.

Peter Manning

other hand she found Elisabeth Schwarzkopf difficult to work with: 'She put me off Wolf for years, although I benefited very much from her teaching later.' Joan performed at the Maltings later in her career and has also herself taught at the School, something she says she loves doing.

The year 1981 ended well and there was a feeling that the School had come of age. The standards of excellence demanded of both the teachers and the students continued to be met; it should always be remembered that these activities were taking place in the unlikely environment of a converted agricultural building in rural Suffolk, surrounded by marshes and water, rutted roads and dilapidated barns.

An enormously important development in the School's history was the link with Jaguar Daimler Cars and the Jaguar Daimler Evenings of Classical Music which took place between 1982 and 1985. In 1981 an advertisement for one of the latest models of a Jaguar car appeared in the press and in selected magazines. The photograph used was one of the latest models of a Jaguar car taken in front of the huge, bronze statue by Henry Moore, *Reclining Figure*, which was on loan from the Moore Foundation and which stood in front of Snape Maltings Concert Hall.

(If only the Henry Moore Foundation had left the statue where it was and not asked for its return in 1987, it might still be in its possession; after it was returned, the statue was the

© Nigel Luckhurst

Galina Vishnevskaya working with soprano Joan Rodgers

It was just out of this world – literally. I loved the feeling of cameraderie and, of course, Peter Pears was an inspiration and Roger Vignoles was always wonderfully helpful.

JOAN RODGERS

subject of a spectacular robbery from the Moore Foundation in Much Hadham, Hertfordshire, in December 2005 and it has never been seen since. It was worth £3 million. In 2009 the police said that the likelihood was that it had been melted down and sold for scrap for £1,500.)

In the early 1980s commercial sponsorship was almost unknown to the School and, indeed, was very much in its infancy as far as the Aldeburgh Foundation was concerned. Rather cheekily, we wrote to Jaguar Cars and suggested that as they had chosen to make such a very obvious link with Snape, perhaps they would be kind enough to lend us a car for the summer courses, in order that the eminent musicians coming to teach could be transported in comfort. We offered to publicize their co-operation in every way we could. Somewhat to our surprise we received a call from John Maries, then and until 2009 Marketing and Promotions Manager for Jaguar Daimler Cars, who agreed to our request.

John Maries was to become a stalwart friend of the Britten–Pears School and of the Festival itself and from the original advertisement and the loan of the car, a very strong relationship between Jaguar Daimler and Aldeburgh was forged. That first summer and for several years following, we had the free use of a luxurious car. When Michael Darlow and Basil Coleman were later filming *The Aldeburgh Story*, a four-part series for Channel 4, a little unofficial 'placement' advertising was arranged; John Owen was to be filmed fetching Suzanne Danco from Pamela Embleton's house in Aldeburgh and, as she emerged, looking as glamorous as usual, to be driven to Snape, she was filmed standing on the steps. Exactly on cue and talking to camera, she asked clearly in her distinctive, accented English, 'John, where is the Jaguar?'

Jaguar Daimler Cars agreed to an annual sponsorship of a concert in the Festival and this relationship led directly to the Daimler Evenings of Classical Music which were to prove a useful showcase for the School and to provide remarkable opportunities, in terms of work and exposure, for the young musicians involved.

The marketing department of Jaguar Daimler Cars had decided that a concert of classical music coupled with a gourmet (well, gourmet-ish) dinner set in a stately home would attract precisely the right target customers and create the right atmosphere for selling their cars. This proved to be a winning formula.

The opportunity to host these events was offered by the company to the dealers nationwide and once it was known which dealerships had accepted, a local stately home would be identified. All the evenings followed an identical pattern: the formally dressed invited guests, typically about a hundred and fifty of them, were met with cocktails followed by a tour of the house. After the tour they listened to the concert and were then conducted to a seated dinner followed by speeches. On some occasions a 'treasure hunt' for a diamond which had been hidden in one of the advertising displays was organized. And the cars sold.

In the initial stages the marketing department of Jaguar Daimler needed to persuade the Chairman, who was then Sir John Egan, that their idea would be successful and John Owen and I were invited to visit him, with John Maries, in his office at Browns Lane, Coventry, to discuss the whole concept and the format for the concerts. The Chairman was extremely welcoming and kind but one had the distinct impression that classical music was not an area of great familiarity to him, an experience that was to be repeated frequently with future sponsors of the Festival. He was very straightforward in his views. 'I want only beautiful music,' he said. We murmured that this was somewhat difficult as ideas of what constituted beautiful music could vary. He said, somewhat impatiently, 'You know perfectly well what I mean. I mean music like *The Four Seasons*.'

We promised to furnish him with beautiful music, to arrange for a talented person of the highest reputation to devise and present the concerts, and that the singers or instrumentalists would be among the most gifted (and attractive – that was important) who had studied or were currently studying at the School. We were confident that we could deliver events of the highest quality that would meet all his demands.

The first series was agreed and the contract signed. We asked Graham Johnson to devise the programme and the first concert took place at Warwick Castle on 23 May 1982 with Cynthia Millar acting as the concert manager. Graham Johnson, Cynthia Millar and the musicians arrived in good time for an early-afternoon rehearsal. John Owen and I got there slightly later, expecting everything to be in order, only to discover total pandemonium, with Cynthia running round frantically in the town looking for the black covers that Graham wanted for the music and Graham himself white-faced with fury as the lighting assistant had not arrived and no one could see to read the music. 'Well,' he said through clenched teeth, 'there just won't be a concert.' This heart-stopping moment threatened the whole project but when the guests arrived all the problems had been solved, miraculously it seemed; no one knew how close we had come to catastrophe.

The programme, which featured music by Schubert and Schumann, was well received and Graham Johnson was, as always, witty and entertaining as a presenter, having written a very elegant script. The audience loved the concert and among the artists taking part were Jane Leslie MacKenzie, the student from Canada, who was expected to go on to a great career but who gave it all up for marriage and children. She was joined by clarinettist Joy Farrall in a performance of Schubert's *Der Hirt auf dem Felsen*.

The concert at Warwick Castle took place early in the year and was deliberately designed as a trial run with a break of several months before the rest of the series was due to take place. This was a sensible plan as it was such a new project for everybody.

Cynthia Millar was unable to continue to manage the concerts as her career as an Ondes Martinot player was beginning to flourish and had to take precedence. Heather Newill, who happened to come into the Aldeburgh office having just finished a freelance cellist job in Germany, arrived at just the right moment: 'Yes, we've got a job for you; you can run the Jaguar concerts.'

She took over and organized all the future events efficiently and smoothly, despite the fact that there always seemed to be problems to be overcome. One of the more dramatic of these was trying (and eventually succeeding) to get a grand piano up a narrow spiral staircase in a Scottish castle. Heather was excellent in the job and later became the Aldeburgh Foundation's concerts manager. She is now a successful head-hunter but she had already had a long association with Aldeburgh, having been the cellist in the Hadow Quartet, which was one of the quartets participating in the very first String Quartet Academies with Cecil Aronowitz and William Pleeth teaching. Heather still talks with great affection and respect for Pleeth: 'He was always so kind.'

Graham Johnson devised the second, equally successful, series, entitled 'Aimez-vous Brahms?', with the Brodsky Quartet and soprano Marilyn Dale. Apart from Warwick Castle, concerts took place at Shugborough, Hopetoun House, Audley End House, Haddon Hall, Ragley Hall, Woburn Abbey, Longleat, Sutton Park, Smithills Hall, Goodwood House and Belvoir Castle.

At the request of the sponsor, two European concerts were added: in the Hotel Europa in Brussels and at the home of the British Ambassador in The Hague, where security was so strict that the only way that the display car could be brought in was over the garden wall, skilfully engineered by Heather Newill.

When the third year's series was mooted, Graham Johnson felt that he could no longer devote enough time to the project and we invited Iain Burnside to present the programmes. To this day Iain quotes me as saying, 'Iain, some people want to look at pretty girls and some people want to look at pretty boys. So please make sure that you cast both.'

Iain Burnside was a regular accompanist for the courses at Snape and, like so many others, he feels that his experience at the School altered and defined his future career. Douglas Boyd, 'part of the Scottish mafia' as Iain says, invited him to come to Snape and play in a charity concert. Peter Pears heard him play the Schubert Impromptu in B flat, which was rather unnerving for Iain. Pears said to him, 'The last person I heard play that was Clifford [Curzon].' But he then went on to say, 'We are looking for accompanists. Would you like to play for some of the courses?' Until then Burnside had been mostly performing in chamber groups and he says that he had never accompanied singers until he came to the School. It is as a vocal accompanist that he became known and one of the fields where he has made a successful career. He also played for some of the String courses and he speaks with enormous respect for William Pleeth from whom he says he learned so much. Burnside also had great personal admiration for Pears and talks of his exquisite manners.

In the Jaguar concerts Iain Burnside proved to be a very talented host. These concerts provided him with his first experience of presentation, which has since led to a second career in the broadcast media, anchoring such high-profile programmes as *BBC Cardiff Singer of the World*.

In all there were forty Jaguar Daimler concerts. The standard of performance was always of the very highest and many of the artists taking part are now household names.

Jaguar Daimler produced very handsome programmes for the concerts with excellent photographs of the relevant stately home and a little piece about each venue. There were the usual programme notes and biographies of the musicians, a piece about the sponsor and the cars and at the end of each programme an enthusiastic piece about the School entitled 'The Snape Story'. It ended: 'The Britten–Pears School for Advanced Musical Studies is an integral part of the Maltings complex and the Concert Hall is now in use for the greater part of the year. Snape Maltings has therefore become not only the home of the Aldeburgh Festival but one of the most important centres for music study and entertainment in Great Britain, its standard of excellence recognized throughout the world.'

One experience with display and sponsorship for Jaguar Cars was not quite so smooth. Sponsorship of a Festival concert had been agreed and everything was in place. Part of the agreement was that Jaguar would floodlight the lawn at Snape in front of the Henry Moore and park three of the latest models there for concert-goers to see as they arrived. The

Iain Burnside accompanying a masterclass for Suzanne Danco

William Pleeth was so inspiring, with such a huge personality and he has left us a huge legacy. He taught the students always to be aware of the interaction between the cello and the keyboard and he used to tell them to listen to the piano.

Peter Pears was always so gracious and had such human generosity. Even if he did not esteem the singer, he always found something positive to say. It was all such a marvellous experience for pianists. The School provided such a wonderful buffer zone between the conservatoires and the harsh realities of professional life.

IAIN BURNSIDE

display was beautifully arranged, the lighting was perfect and the floodlit cars lined up on the lawn were impressive and stylish. Parking was always a problem at Snape concerts and on this particular evening Donald Mitchell, driving an old and rather battered car, arrived at the Hall later than he expected and was absolutely delighted to see what he thought was a new car park specially waiting for him. He was not at all pleased to be asked to move his car and I don't think that he ever fully understood why his parking arrangements caused such consternation. The incident cannot have done anything to counteract his inherent distaste for commercial sponsorship.

The concept of the 'Daimler Evening of Classical Music' was so successful and at the same time so beneficial for the School that when we were subsequently asked by Chesterton's in London to devise a programme for the company, using exactly the same formula, we were very happy to agree. The presenter on this occasion was violinist Gonzalo Acosta, and Alastair Creamer was the concert manager, with Alison Hagley as one of the singers.

As far as the staff were concerned we were doing something entirely beneficial for the School. The sponsor was very happy and we were providing the students with opportunities for work that could only enhance their reputations. But the project came in for criticism and some Trustees of the Britten–Pears Foundation were very disapproving, considering that it was all far too commercial and removed from the original ideals of the School. I must say that Peter Pears himself was not among them and he thoroughly supported what we were doing and – ever the pragmatist – delighted in the fact that the students were being given paid work.

I had by this time left the School staff and been appointed Head of Development for the Aldeburgh Foundation. We were starting a campaign to obtain commercial sponsorship for the Festival and, of course, for the School. This was an area in which no one then had any experience but which was obviously essential for a perpetually cash-strapped organization.

Our sponsorship campaign, after a faltering start, flourished, despite the fact that half of our catchment area was in the North Sea and catering was a permanent problem. It remained our Achilles heel. One difficulty was that we really had no suitable space for entertaining and although we decided that a large marquee would be a solution for receptions during the Festival, this was not entirely satisfactory.

George Gooderham, the owner of the whole complex, including the Concert Hall which we only leased, was also in charge of all the catering. Although he was always co-operative and anxious to do his best, he was not a professional caterer. The whole business tended to be a nerve-racking and hit-and-miss affair. I remember John Gummer, who as our local Member of Parliament was a wonderful and loyal supporter, memorably saying, rather sorrowfully, 'Gnawing an under-cooked chicken leg in a badly lit marquee is not really the answer.' Over the years we were to suffer several disasters and near disasters.

Eastern Gas, one of our sponsors, did not consider the light food provided sufficient sustenance for hungry Eastern Gas customers who had missed their tea, and the managers were enraged when, inexplicably and to my utter astonishment, George Gooderham, in a genuine attempt to please, provided for their reception only meringues and little cakes.

But undoubtedly the worst experience was the sponsorship by a high-street bank, including a concert in the Snape Proms, with the post-concert reception taking place in the Recital Room of the School. The previous year the bank had sponsored 'An Evening of Viennese Music', all swirling skirts and waltzes, which they loved and which they wanted to repeat. However, in the following year's programme there was to be no Viennese evening; in its place was a concert entitled 'Cabaret' with saxophonist John Harle. It was thought that this would fit the bill. I demurred but I was overruled and told that they would thoroughly enjoy the programme. I was right; they didn't like the idea at all. It took a great deal of persuasion and much rather gabbled talk of Liza Minnelli to get them to agree.

How I was to wish that they hadn't! The first half of the concert consisted of *very* loud jazz and music composed by John Harle himself; the connection with Kander's and Ebb's *Cabaret* was tenuous indeed. From the back of the hall I was dismayed to see the sponsor's guests covering their ears and removing their hearing aids. The second half was, if anything, even more challenging – although I must admit there was a small piece of the well-known *Cabaret* film music included.

After it ended a furious manager hissed at me as we made our way to the reception, 'Well, Moira, the party had better be good.'

What I didn't know as I came out of the Concert Hall was that the person George Gooderham had put in charge of the catering had apparently suffered a breakdown of some sort earlier in the evening and had simply put on his coat and run away from the kitchen, leaving no instructions for the staff. This was the stuff of nightmares and I desperately hoped that I would soon wake up. In the Recital Room where everything should have been ready for a party, there were three bare trestle tables with not a *single* thing on them, not even tablecloths, and sixty hungry, thirsty and angry sponsor's guests, still nursing their painful ears.

No one has ever gone up the stairs to the prep rooms more quickly than I did that evening but all I could find were some catering-size bags of crisps. Better than nothing, but not really sufficient to placate the bank's guests. Unbelievably, worse was to follow. Before the concert and before I realized how much the sponsor would dislike the programme, I had invited John Harle and the other musicians to come to the reception and stressed how important their presence would be for the sponsor and his guests. This proved to be a big mistake. John Harle dutifully arrived and was introduced to the Regional Manager who, although still decidedly cross, made a noble effort to be polite and friendly, even though it was through gritted teeth.

'Oh, I see you were at the Albert Hall the other night.' (This was shortly after the building's refurbishment.) 'How did you find it?'

'I went to South Kensington tube station and walked up Exhibition Road,' John Harle replied, smiling his affable and warmly sociable smile.

In the circumstances it was hardly surprising that the sponsor responded with a short Anglo-Saxon phrase.

This particular sponsorship was not repeated but, despite such a spectacular setback, support for the Festival and the Proms grew and as we all began to understand the importance of a relationship with the commercial world. At the same time sponsorship at the School grew in parallel; 'education' and 'social responsibility' were now buzz words on the sponsorship scene.

Times were changing and the opportunity to entertain commercial clients was ceasing to be the foremost reason for sponsoring the arts. This new trend benefited the School. BP became a regular School sponsor, as did other East Anglian and national companies, but no one else, apart from Jaguar Daimler Cars and Chesterton's, took advantage of the opportunities that private concerts provided and which we knew had given the School welcome additional publicity and from which all the students taking part had gained, both financially and in terms of experience.

The foundations laid in the three years since the School had been working in its new building proved solid and the 1982 season of courses was to be equally successful although eventful both in the history of the Foundation and of the School too.

The School personnel again underwent a change. After I left the staff and was appointed Head of Development for the Foundation, John Owen became the Administrator of the School with overall responsibility for all the courses and all aspects of the administration. Alastair Creamer joined as an assistant and blew into all our lives rather like a whirlwind. Clever, funny, enthusiastic and efficient, he was a very popular member of staff and after two years became the Concerts Manager for the Foundation.

But there were far greater changes in the Foundation itself. After the resignation of Sir Eugene Melville from the chairmanship, Lord Inverforth became the Chairman, but he died tragically and unexpectedly after serving for only a short period. Peter Bowring, who had for a long time been a member of the Council, now became the Chairman.

Jack Phipps had been the General Manager for a year and during that time had overseen such an enormous increase in the Foundation's deficit that it was hovering on the brink of bankruptcy. This was not exactly surprising given that in the 1982 Festival there was the vast expense of two performances of *The Beggar's Opera* by Kent Opera and two performances by Sadler's Wells Royal Ballet. There was a very real possibility that

This was my second 'proper' job and I was still fresh and green behind the ears. But I learned so much. I learned how to treat people with attention and generosity. I learned about quality and excellence. And among this I developed a deep connection with Britten's music. Even now his music takes me back to the pebble beach at Aldeburgh, the Jubilee Hall, the porch of the School, the John Pipers on the wall and Peter Pears sitting in the Recital Room. My artistic memories are of the operas produced at the School during my time there, The Turn of the Screw *and* Owen Wingrave.

I marvel at people's trust and the levels of delegation. I was allowed to stage manage, to design props and scenery and even to re-create the flags for Owen Wingrave *under the watchful eye of John Piper, who sat in on rehearsals.*

That's what the School did for people – gave them creative energy and then released them. By and large, we've flown. My life really kick-started at Aldeburgh and it has been a constant reference point for me ever since.

ALASTAIR CREAMER

we would be unable to continue trading and the astounding achievements of the Festival and the School would have been brought to an end. In October 1982 Phipps resigned. The full story of the circumstances of his resignation can be read in Peter Bowring's book, *The Last Minute*.

Kenneth Baird, appointed Concerts Manager by Phipps only six months previously, became the new General Manager and it can be fairly said that his appointment saved the Aldeburgh Foundation.

The greatest contribution he made to solving the dire financial circumstances in which the Foundation found itself, apart from immediately cancelling a proposed and very costly performance of *Parsifal* that Phipps had negotiated, was his masterly negotiation with the Central Electricity Generating Board over the leasing of the Concert Hall and the ancillary buildings, including the School, for the Public Enquiry into the Sizewell B Nuclear Power Station.

Sir Frank Layfield had been appointed to conduct the Public Enquiry into the potential siting of a second nuclear power station at Sizewell, the tiny hamlet on the Suffolk coast near Leiston. A suitably large hall for the Enquiry itself and offices for all the staff were required. The Snape Maltings Concert Hall complex was ideal. The Enquiry proved to be the longest-running public enquiry ever held in England to date and lasted from 1983 to 1985. The rental received over this three-year period was to provide the Foundation with an essential financial cushion.

Isador Caplan, Britten's lawyer and a Trustee of the Britten–Pears Foundation, had been in discussion with the CEGB and was able to give Kenneth Baird excellent advice. However, in the event Baird carried out all the negotiations and when the initial lease came up for renewal, he conducted the second round of negotiations and gained substantially increased rental for the Foundation.

The lease with the CEGB allowed the Festival to take place in the Maltings, but it meant that the Concert Hall was unavailable for the rest of the year; as was the School building, which was needed by the CEGB for its administrative offices.

It was very inconvenient and poignant that, so soon after moving into its own building, the School was forced to relocate to various halls and spaces in Aldeburgh. It was a small price to pay for the continuing existence of the entire organization, but it was very difficult for the School staff. In 1983 and 1984 masterclasses were held in the Jubilee Hall, in the Baptist Chapel and in private houses in and around Aldeburgh.

Baird not only understood the need for financial rigour but, free from the suspicion and distrust that had bedevilled the administration in recent years, he became a first-class administrator of a complicated undertaking. He worked extremely well with Peter Pears and the other Artistic Directors, with the Trustees of the Britten–Pears Foundation and with the Council of the Aldeburgh Foundation. He made some excellent appointments and was popular with the staff; after the turmoil of the previous months everything settled down and both the

Foundation and the School looked forward to a calm period of development despite the problems posed by the Sizewell Enquiry. Baird understood that the School, under Owen's skilful management, had developed into an efficient and well-run organization and, although he had overall responsibility for the whole operation, he was happy to allow the School to run itself; while being wholly supportive, he did not interfere in its day-to-day activities. It should be understood that, although he was happy to let the staff at the School get on with the work, he was, from the outset, aware that a higher degree of integration needed to be established between the management of the School and the management of the Concert Hall.

Before Jack Phipps's resignation it had been decided to launch an Appeal for a capital fund to make certain improvements to the Concert Hall and to benefit the School. We were fortunate that Sir Richard Cave, a leading industrialist – the founding Chairman of Thorn EMI, Deputy Chairman of British Rail and Chairman of Vickers – who had a house in Aldeburgh, agreed to become the Chairman of the Appeal. He gathered around him a team of real heavyweights who were to prove hard working and invaluable in helping us to reach the target, which was set at £1 million. This may now seem to be quite a modest sum, but in 1982, and in Aldeburgh, it was a large amount. The Vice-Presidents, who were all there at the personal invitation of Sir Richard, could hardly have been more distinguished or in a better position to ensure the success of the Appeal.

COURSES FOR SINGERS 1983

	Monday 25	Tuesday 26	Wednesday 27	Thursday 28
	9.15 REGISTRATION AND INTRODUCTION FOLLOWED BY COFFEE 10.00 Visit to Britten-Pears Library	9.00–10.15 Practice	9.00–9.30 Practice 9.45–10.15 WARM UP JH Nancy Evans	9.00–10.15 Practice
10.30		COFFEE	COFFEE	COFFEE
11.00	11.00–12.00 Practice 12.15–12.45 WARM UP JH Nancy Evans	MASTER CLASS Kerstin Meyer AC	MASTER CLASS Kerstin Meyer JH	MASTER CLASS Kerstin Meyer JH
1.00	LUNCH	LUNCH	LUNCH	LUNCH
2.15 -4.15	DICTION CLASS Kerstin Meyer JH	CONSULTS P Pears N Evans RH	CONSULTS P Pears N Evans RH	CONSULTS P Pears N Evans RH
4.30	TEA	TEA	TEA	TEA
5.00 -7.00	MASTER CLASS Kerstin Meyer JH	MASTER CLASS Kerstin Meyer JH	MASTER CLASS Kerstin Meyer JH	MASTER CLASS Kerstin Meyer JH

Daily schedule at the School during the Sizewell B Enquiry, showing classes taking place in the Jubilee Hall, the Red House and the Aldeburgh Cinema

Aldeburgh Foundation Appeal 1986

Sir Richard Cave
Chairman

Appeal Committee
David Barclay
Barclays Bank
Peter Bowring
Chairman CT Bowring Ltd
William Jacob
Aldeburgh Foundation Council member
Cyril Russell
lawyer and Aldeburgh resident
Sidney Spiro
banker
Sir Peter Walters
Chairman of BP

Moira Bennett
Secretary

At a meeting of the Council, Sir Richard asked, 'What do the staff call the Aldeburgh Festival–Snape Maltings Foundation?'

'The Aldeburgh Foundation' was the reply.

'Right, that's what it will be called from now on.'

This was typical of Sir Richard Cave and so 'The Aldeburgh Foundation' it became, which was not only an improvement in general but very much easier for running an appeal. Cave realized very early on that people were far more likely to donate money if education was seen as the main thrust of the campaign and consequently the focus of the appeal became the School.

I was the Secretary to the Appeal Committee and Dick Cave – as we came to know him – was a wonderful man to work for. He was probably one of the busiest men in the country, but, nevertheless, he was never too busy to give advice and practical help nor to surrender his precious weekends for the Appeal. Tragically, Dick died in 1986 after a distressing illness but the Appeal was successful and the Britten–Pears School owes him an enormous debt of gratitude.

In his memory Vickers made a donation of £50,000 and this was the impetus for an annual Festival concert given by the Britten–Pears Orchestra (the successor to the Snape Maltings Training Orchestra) sponsored by Gillian Cave, Dick's widow.

The more musically and artistically inclined among the leading personalities connected with Aldeburgh were very grateful to Dick Cave for raising the money that was so badly needed, and for making the School the focus of the Appeal. There were, however, undercurrents of suspicion and some resentment that the Foundation should be dependent on the fundraising efforts of these captains of industry who were secretly, perhaps, slightly despised.

Equally, in conversations I had with the industrialists and business leaders, I felt often that there was no real understanding of the true aims and the value of the School. They helped simply because Dick Cave asked them to do so and, because they were competitive people, it became a matter of pride to raise more money than their fellow Vice-Presidents. Some members – such as Bishop Allison and Billy Burrell – were there simply to represent Aldeburgh residents and were not expected to raise money. Although the majority of the Vice-Presidents made a real effort, there were others who, to Dick Cave's intense irritation, did little to help but seemed to like having their names included.

The School programme continued and in March 1982 there was a weekend course focusing on the music of Hans Werner Henze, with the composer himself directing the course, assisted by Jan Latham-Koenig. Henze's rather flamboyant lifestyle contrasted sharply with the rural Suffolk environment but the course was a great success and his presence was certainly a feather in the School's cap.

The Vice-Presidents included:

The Right Reverend Faulkner Allison
formerly Bishop of Winchester; Aldeburgh resident

Peter Andry
record producer; Manager, EMI International Artists

Billy Burrell
friend of Benjamin Britten and legendary Aldeburgh fisherman

Lord Delfont
impressario; Chairman and CEO, EMI Films and Theatre Corporation

Sir Kenneth Durham Chairman, Unilever

Sir Peter Green Chairman, Lloyds of London

Philip Greenwell stockbroker

The Hon. Alan Hare Chairman, The Financial Times

John Harvey Jones Chairman, ICI

Andrew Lloyd Webber composer

Sir Godfrey Messervy Chairman, Lucas Industries

Sir Ian Morrow management consultant

Richard Pears
second cousin of Peter Pears; Manager, The Dairy Marketing Board

Sir Patrick Sergeant
City Editor, The Daily Mail and President, Euromoney

Sir Gerald Thorley Chairman, Allied Breweries

Sam Toy
Chairman and Managing Director, Ford Motor Co.

Sir Ian Trethowan
Director General, BBC

© Eric Richmond

The present-day Brodsky Quartet: Daniel Rowland and Ian Belton (violins), Paul Cassidy (viola), Jacqueline Thomas (cello)

This course was followed immediately by a Solo Viola course which was to have been given by Gérard Caussé and William Primrose with Nicola Grunberg as accompanist. Primrose had accepted the invitation, but died shortly before the course was to start. Hugh Maguire telephoned all the students, who were, of course, very upset by the news of Primrose's death, and told them to come as a substitute teacher had been found: the respected player Donald McInnes, himself a former pupil of Primrose.

There were nine students on the course, including Paul Cassidy, who had been on many courses at Snape, was a member of the BPO and had recently joined the Brodsky Quartet. The Quartet had been formed in 1972 when its members were all still children and in 1982 the same original four were still members. That year the viola player, Alex Robertson, decided to leave. Hugh Maguire was asked to suggest a replacement. Hugh recommended Paul Cassidy.

In April there was the annual Academy of String Quartets with the Vermeer Quartet (Shmuel Ashkenazi, Pierre Menard, Bernard Zaslav and Marc Johnson). There were eleven quartets invited on to this course after fierce competition, including the Alexandra, the Colorado, the Fairfield and the Hanson Quartets, returning to the Academy after study at Snape in earlier years.

April saw another course – Roles from Britten Operas – with Peter Pears, Nancy Evans, Steuart Bedford, Eric Crozier and Colin Graham as faculty members, and accompanists

Continued on page 144

I shall never forget that course, which completely changed my life. We had three days of marvellous teaching from Caussé, this elegant European, and then suddenly there was Donald McInnes – American, dressed casually, friendly and utterly different. After my first class, he came up to me and asked, 'What are you doing this summer?' Well, I was a student; not only did I have no plans but the summer seemed a lifetime away. 'Would you like to come and study with me in Santa Barbara? It's three months.' I was astonished and then he gave me a form to complete and actually got me a full scholarship. I went to America to study with him for three months. But something else happened then that also profoundly affected my future.

When Cecil Aronowitz collapsed while playing in the Maltings Concert Hall his viola was smashed to pieces. Charles Beare did his best to repair it. After it was mended, Nicola Grunberg, Aronowitz's widow, telephoned Brian Hawkins at the Royal College of Music with whom I was studying and as a result of this conversation, I was offered the loan of the viola.

At the end of the course there was a concert in the Maltings and I was chosen to play Britten's Lachrymae *as the last item. Nickie Grunberg was the pianist. You can imagine the atmosphere. Here I was playing Britten's* Lachrymae *on Cecil Aronowitz's viola accompanied by Cecil's widow. It was a sold-out house and Peter Pears was sitting in the front row and he was overcome by emotion. It was all too much for me and after*

Paul Cassidy with the Bridge–Britten viola in the Britten–Pears Library

the concert, I went backstage and simply walked out. I felt I had to be alone.

The next day when I returned everyone asked where I had been. 'Peter Pears wants to see you at the Red House.' I was very anxious. What had I done? I was taken to the Red House and Peter greeted me at the door and took me inside. He pointed to a box under the piano and told me to get it out. I opened the box and inside was a bow held together with Sellotape which was old and brown and under a red silk scarf was a viola which was almost black and had one string. But it had a gorgeous scroll.

'I have been told that you don't have an instrument,' Peter said. 'Would you like it? Your performance last night was very beautiful and I'd like you to have it.' I was utterly flabbergasted. I hardly knew what to say. The viola, which was Britten's [and formerly Frank Bridge's], went to Charles Beare who cleaned it up and did an amazing job on it.

In November 1986, four years later and, of course, after Peter's death, the Quartet was playing in a Britten concert at the Wigmore Hall and when we finished and came off, we went into the Green Room. I hadn't even put the instrument away when a voice behind me said, 'Mr Cassidy? I am Isador Caplan, a Britten Trustee. You have something belonging to us and we want it back.' People were starting to come into the Green Room and I felt as though I was being accused of theft.

It was a very serious situation. We had a busy concert programme and I would have nothing to play on. I wasn't going to say, 'But Peter Pears gave it to me', so I wrote to as many people as I could, people that I thought would have influence, and I am happy to say that eventually I got a nice letter saying that I could keep the instrument.

Aldeburgh was the greatest influence on my life. I became a member of the Brodsky Quartet through Aldeburgh; I went to America as a result of studying at Snape, and I was given Britten's viola there. The place has completely shaped my life.

PAUL CASSIDY

© Nigel Luckhurst

Peter Pears

Façade
Music by William Walton   Texts by Edith Sitwell

Aldeburgh Festival 1982

Nancy Evans   Richard Baker   readers
Jonathan Burgess flute/piccolo
Richard Hosford clarinet/bass clarinet
Nigel Scragg alto saxophone
Geoffrey Harniess trumpet
William Conway   Rhydian Shaxson   cellos
William Lockhart percussion
Conducted by Hugh Maguire

Drapers' Hall 1985

Nancy Evans   Richard Baker   readers
Simon Channing flute/piccolo
Joy Farrall clarinet/bass clarinet
Martin Robertson alto saxophone
Jeremy Banks trumpet
Nicholas Roberts   Robert Irvine   cellos
William Lockhart percussion
Conducted by Hugh Maguire

Richard Balcombe, Nancy Cooley, Stephen Rose and Stephen Westrop. This was followed by a Lute and English Song course with Pears, Evans and Robert Spencer. The accompanists were pianists Richard Balcombe, Ronald Lumsden, and David Mason and lutenists Philip Dunn and Dorothy Linnell.

A Walton Symposium directed by Donald Mitchell, with Victoria Glendinning, Arnold Whittall and Gillian Widdicombe, took place in June and included a visit from Lady Walton. Victoria Glendinning had recently published a biography of Edith Sitwell and her insights into the poet's work were invaluable during rehearsals for the performances of *Façade* in the Festival and later (in 1985) in the Drapers' Hall in London as a fund-raiser for the Aldeburgh Appeal.

The 1982 School programme followed the established pattern with the SMTO performing in the Festival, conducted by George Malcolm and with Carmen Pelton (for the indisposed Joan Rodgers) singing the Mozart concert aria 'Ch'io mi scordi di te' ((K. 505). There followed courses on French Song with Hugues Cuénod; Bach and Handel with John Carol Case, Ilse Wolf and Paul Esswood; in August German Song with Kerstin Meyer and Thomas Hemsley, and Chamber Music with William Pleeth, Hugh Maguire and Norbert Brainin.

After this came a Piano Trio course with Hugh Maguire, William Pleeth and Artur Balsam. On this course there were twelve trios, including the Burnside Trio with Iain Burnside, Wendy Sharp and Sally-Jane Pendlebury; the Drake Trio with Julius Drake, Jacqueline Shave and Rachel Maguire, and the

Lockhart Trio with Robert Lockhart, Catherine Lord and Tim Hugh.

The September SMTO course had Artur Balsam as soloist and the conducting was shared between Murray Perahia, Hugh Maguire and Antal Dorati. In October a course on the Britten Song-Cycles was held with students Helen Charnock, Ian Christopher, Amelia Fonti and Mark Tucker and accompanist Julius Drake.

This was another excellent year for the School. The staff, led by John Owen and Virginia Caldwell, with Alastair Creamer and Susan Wilson as assistants, was settled and confident. The pattern of established courses proved successful and the auditioning process had produced the right results.

In April 1983 courses began with an English Song course and a French Song course. Peter Pears and Nancy Evans led the English Song course; consultations, held in Red Studio, beside the Red House, were with Joan Cross and Rae Woodland. Hugues Cuénod had been booked for the French Song course but at the last moment he was forced to cancel and it was extremely fortunate that in his place Gérard Souzay, one of the world's leading exponents of French song, agreed to come to Snape and join Pears and Evans.

In May preparations began for the Aldeburgh Festival performances of *The Turn of the Screw*. This represented a sea change in the relationship between the School and the Festival. Although students from the School had previously been

© Nigel Luckhurst

Hugues Cuénod with Amelia Fonti

© Nigel Luckhurst

The Turn of the Screw: Anna Steiger as Miss Jessel and Lynne Dawson as the Governess

engaged for Festival performances and there was a regular SMTO concert in the Festival programme, there had never been a complete opera produced and performed by the School.

This was Kenneth Baird's first Festival as General Manager and the financial crisis he had inherited was still an unavoidable consideration in the Festival planning. At an early stage it was realized that a professional opera company was financially out of the question and the decision was taken to present School performances as part of the Festival. Baird saw this development as part of the closer and beneficial association he had envisaged between Snape Maltings Concert Hall and the School that would offer unique performance opportunities for the students.

At this period, the Aldeburgh Foundation and the Britten–Pears School were becoming a perfect model of a cultural organization in the round, with an extensive educational aspect and strong links with its local community. Baird was also involved in positive discussions with the local authorities in the area. *Snape Sounds for Schools*, a collaboration between the Local Education Authority and the Aldeburgh Foundation was one of the first fruits of this dialogue.

There was, at a later stage, criticism from some quarters of the decision to include a student opera in the Festival; the accusation was that in making use of the School in this way, the Festival was taking advantage of 'cheap' labour. The benefit to the students far outweighed any other consideration. *The Turn of the Screw* marked a watershed in the growth of the School and was to set a pattern for the future. Opera courses in the ensuing years provided the singers from the School and the members of the orchestra with professional experience, exposure to a discerning audience and the press, all of which was to prove invaluable in their careers. It also presented the School with an enormous and exciting new challenge.

Many of the singers had been regular students at the School and had had the benefit of attending a number of courses. Anna Steiger was the daughter of actors Rod Steiger and Claire Bloom, who were intensely supportive of her career, attended many of the masterclasses, and were familiar figures at the School.

There was no set as such and Bob Ling cleverly constructed a backdrop from the flats; this meant that everything depended on the lighting, which was brilliantly conceived by Roger Weaver, the Foundation's long-serving lighting designer. Costumes were lent by English National Opera.

The name of the School orchestra was changed in 1983 from the Snape Maltings Training Orchestra to the Britten–Pears Orchestra. For the *Turn of the Screw* performances it was led by Brian Brooks and the orchestra list contains the names of Douglas Boyd, Richard Hosford, Ursula Leveaux, Jacqueline Shave and Robert Winn. John Owen was always very protective of the BPO. Pursuing the vision of Cecil Aronowitz, he insisted that it should always be seen as a training orchestra. The central aim was for the young players to gain experience and to work under the finest international conductors.

Britten: The Turn of the Screw
Aldeburgh Festival, 1983

Prologue	Ian Christopher
	Stanley Warren
The Governess	Helen Charnock
	Lynne Dawson
Miles	Adam Ashton
	Martin Phipps
Flora	Maria Bovino
	Mary Seers
Mrs Grose	Marion Olsen
	Anne Todd
Quint	Ian Christopher
	Stanley Warren
Miss Jessel	Anna Steiger
	Marcia Swanston

Britten–Pears Orchestra
Leader Brian Brooks
Conducted by George Malcolm
Directed by Basil Coleman
Lighting Design by Roger Weaver

© Nigel Luckhurst

The Turn of the Screw: Flora (Maria Bovino) in the schoolroom

The production of *The Turn of the Screw* was supported by Adnams Brewery. Simon Loftus, Executive Chairman of Adnams Brewery in Southwold, was an enthusiastic and valued supporter of both the Festival and the School and made a significant contribution to the School's development. He was a regular and informed observer of the masterclasses and later became a member of the Aldeburgh Foundation Council.

Donald Mitchell gave a lecture entitled '*The Turn of the Screw*: Opera as Chamber Music' and there was a discussion forum, chaired by Mitchell, with Joan Cross (the original Mrs Grose), Peter Pears (the original Quint), Myfanwy Piper (the opera's librettist), John Piper, who had designed the set for the first production, and Basil Coleman, director of the School's production and of the opera's 1954 premiere. John Piper's work, including his sketch for the *Turn of the Screw* set, from the Britten–Pears collection formed the Festival exhibition.

Witold Lutosławski was in Aldeburgh for the Festival and the School presented 'Lutoslawski and Szymanowski' with soprano Lynne Dawson and mezzo-soprano Marcia Swanston, with Iain Burnside (piano), Alastair Miles (flute), Nicholas Daniel (oboe), Joy Farrall and Derek Hannigan (clarinets) and Ursula Leveaux (bassoon). It was a remarkable line-up.

The Britten–Pears Orchestra conducted by Lutosławski also gave a concert during the Festival. It was led on this occasion by Andrew Roberts, later one of the founders of the Chamber Orchestra of Europe and a member of the Orchestra of the Age of Enlightenment. The programme included a performance of

Lutosławski's *Paroles tissées*, with Adrian Thompson as the tenor soloist, and the Double Concerto for oboe, harp and chamber orchestra with Nicholas Daniel (oboe) and Eleri Davies (harp).

Following the success of the School's Festival events, the schedule of courses was resumed with John Shirley-Quirk giving masterclasses for a Bach course and Kerstin Meyer directing a Scandinavian Song course. In August, Singers courses included a German Song course with Thomas Hemsley and a Russian Song course with Galina Vishnevskaya.

The German Song course was the first on which Ethna Robinson was a student. Her teacher in Ireland, Nancy Calthorpe, was a regular observer on the Singers courses and she had brought her pupil with her in 1981 and 1982. Nancy Calthorpe asked Peter Pears whether he would hear Ethna Robinson sing. He recognized her potential immediately and recommended that she apply for courses the following year.

In 1984, when the School opera production was Britten's *Owen Wingrave*, Ethna Robinson was cast as Kate. She was heard by a representative of English National Opera, who put her in touch with the company where she was auditioned. As a result she was offered a contract and made her debut at ENO in *Madame Butterfly*. Robinson was then offered the part of Hansel, a role in which she was a triumph, in the award-winning David Pountney production of *Hansel and Gretel*, which was televised by the BBC. She is now recognised as one of the leading British-based character mezzos.

Kerstin Meyer

© Nigel Luckhurst

Galina Vishnevskaya

The role that Galina Vishnevskaya played in the School has already been described by Stephen Ralls and Bruce Ubukata (see pp. 62–4). The Russian Song courses were to become a central part of the School year and at that time Vishnevskaya, formerly the prima donna of the Bolshoi Opera, gave master-classes nowhere else.

I went to visit Galina Vishnevskaya in 2008 in Moscow where she now runs her own opera school. It is situated in a beautiful city-centre house which has been converted into administrative offices, practice rooms, rehearsal studios and a beautiful little opera house. Galina herself lives in an apartment at the top of the building. She still feels keenly the loss of Mstislav Rostropovich who died of cancer in Moscow in 2007 and the seat next to her in the hall is always kept empty – 'for Slava'.

I travelled to Moscow with Nick Winter, a fluent Russian speaker, who used to work at the School and afterwards for the Foundation itself. With us also was Oleg Kogan, the Russian cellist who had studied at the Moscow Conservatory and is now the Director of the Razumovsky Ensemble and the Razumovsky Academy. Galina invited us to the Finals of her Singers Competition which was held in the stunning new Moscow Concert Hall, overlooking the river, and afterwards to a reception. The seat next to her at the reception, too, was kept empty – Slava's seat.

Vishnevskaya talked to me of her days at Snape and of her great admiration and affection for Britten and Pears. She remembered many of her students and particularly talked about what she called 'the unique atmosphere created around Ben and Peter'.

Vishnevskaya talked about a performance of a Tchaikovsky duet she had sung with Pears, with Britten accompanying them and asked whether a recording had been made of it. (Tchaikovsky made sketches for a duet based in part on the Overture to *Romeo and Juliet* for soprano, tenor and orchestra; it was completed by his pupil, Sergei Taneyev, in 1894.) 'How I'd love to have that recording. Peter had huge music in front, written in huge letters – he wanted to sing without glasses!'

It was wonderful to see the affection and regard she retained for the School and how clear her memories were of the students she had taught there. There is no doubt that she is devoted to her school in Moscow, preparing singing students for professional careers on the stage, and has been very much influenced by her experience at Snape.

After the 1983 Singers courses, courses for Solo Strings were held with William Pleeth and Norbert Brainin of the Amadeus Quartet giving masterclasses. String courses ended with the Academy of String Quartets led by the La Salle Quartet.

The School year ended in October with a Mozart and J. C. Bach course directed by Elisabeth Schwarzkopf.

In March 1984 Imogen Holst died at her home in Aldeburgh. Peter Pears wrote, 'She lived and worked in Aldeburgh for the last thirty years of her life, a familiar figure in the High Street, and much loved and admired for her kindness, enthusiasm and

© Nigel Luckhurst

Galina Vishnevskaya

From my point of view the School should exist. It's unique. But it should have the personalities on the same level of great artists as before. You can't create the environment without that. It may have changed but one hopes it will happen again. But life in general has changed and perhaps young people don't want to study singing in quite the same way. They need these personalities whom they can emulate.

GALINA VISHNEVSKAYA

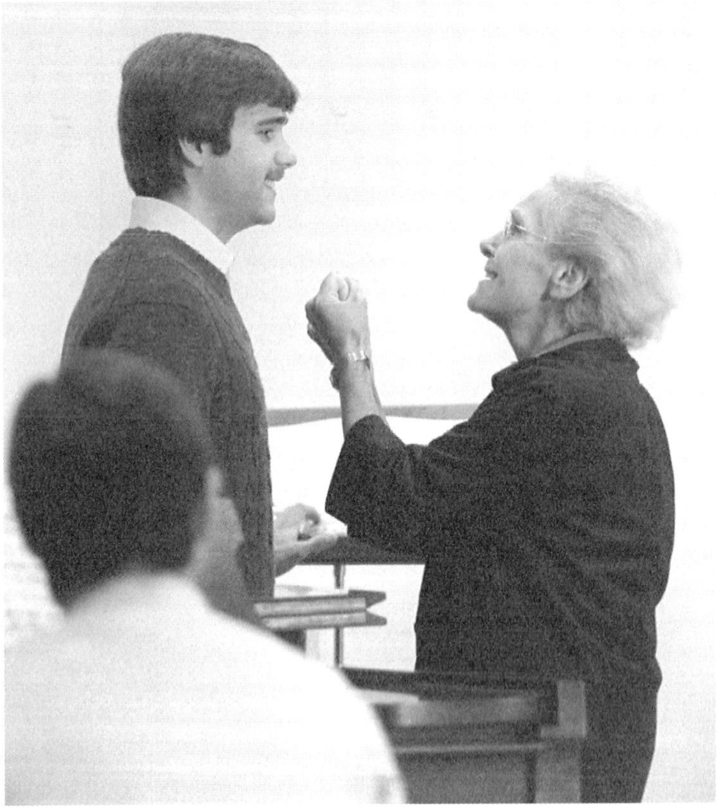

© Nigel Luckhurst

© Nigel Luckhurst

Elisabeth Schwarzkopf with Stanley Warren

wit.' Malcolm Williamson, Master of the Queen's Music, was quoted as saying, 'She was one of the world's great teachers and was able to communicate to all who met her her knowledge and love of music and exactly what she required from her players and singers . . . It seems so incredible that one so full of the Joy of Life has left us – in the flesh – but I feel sure her spirit is with us – unless she is too busy arranging the angelic music of Heaven.'

Imogen Holst had been a cornerstone in the vision and development of the Britten–Pears School and her death brought a sense of loss felt by all associated with the School. The Brindisi Quartet (Jacqueline Shave, Patrick Kiernan, Katie Wilkinson and Robert Irvine), which had been formed through meeting at the School and which went on to such success, performed at her Memorial Concert in Thaxted Church.

The highlight of the 1984 School year was the production of the opera *Owen Wingrave*. Benjamin Britten's surviving Executors, Peter Pears, Isador Caplan (with his wife Joan a dedicatee of the opera) and Donald Mitchell, wrote in the Festival programme, '*Owen Wingrave*, the Britten opera that is being performed at this year's Festival, takes an unequivocal stand against the spirit of militarism and offers a realistic concept of peace as something – to quote Owen's words – that is "not lazy but vigilant . . . not acquiescent but searching . . . Peace is not silent, it is the voice of love".'

The set designed by John Piper for the first staged performances of the opera – a large metal framework – was kindly

© Nigel Luckhurst

Owen Wingrave: Owen's vision of battle

Owen Wingrave: Jennifer Bolam (Kate) and James Meek (Owen)

Owen Wingrave: John Oakley Tucker (Owen), and (seated) Tracey Chadwell (Mrs Julian), Robert Craig (Lechmere) and Deirdre Crowley (Mrs Coyle)

loaned by the Royal Opera House (as were some of the costumes) and no one will ever forget the day it arrived and had to be installed on the stage of the Maltings. 'It won't fit,' was Bob Ling's unequivocal verdict when he saw the set unloaded and for one dreadful moment this certainly seemed to be true. To this day Kenneth Baird and Alastair Creamer recall the horror of the moment when it was realized that it really might not be possible to get the set on to the stage. In fact, against all the odds, the set was put into place with precisely one inch to spare on either side.

Myfanwy Piper, the librettist of *Owen Wingrave*, which is based on a story by Henry James, was at Snape for rehearsals. The School was wonderfully fortunate in having not only John Piper's set but he, himself, present and ready to give advice and help with the production. Edward Piper, their son, designed the portraits of the Wingrave family for the set, as he had done at the Royal Opera House.

Owen Wingrave followed the pattern that had been established in 1983 with the School production of *The Turn of the Screw* and the School presenting opera in the Aldeburgh Festival at a professional level; it was an unqualified success.

The Britten–Pears Orchestra gave a concert in the Festival with Radu Lupu playing Beethoven's Third Piano Concerto. Toru Takemitsu was the composer-in-residence in 1984 and included in the BPO programme was his *Toward the Sea* (a first British performance) with soloists from the School: Robert Winn (flute) and Imogen Barford (harp). There was also a

Britten: Owen Wingrave
Aldeburgh Festival, 1984

Owen Wingrave	James Meek
	John Oakley Tucker
Spencer Coyle	Gary Coward
	Duncan Smith
Lechmere	Neill Archer
	Robert Craig
Miss Wingrave	Marcia Swanston
	Anne Todd
Mrs Coyle	Helen Charnock
	Deirdre Crowley
Mrs Julian	Louise Camens
	Tracey Chadwell
Kate Julian	Jennifer Bolam
	Ethna Robinson
General Sir Philip Wingrave	James Leatch
Narrator	Martin Spencer

The Britten–Pears Orchestra
Leader Brian Brooks

Conducted by Steuart Bedford
Directed by Basil Coleman
Lighting Design by Roger Weaver

I was treated with such respect and learned so much. I sometimes heard students bickering and complaining that in order to succeed at Snape you had to be a part of a clique but that was certainly not my experience. Until then I had been working on the baroque repertoire but both Jan de Gaetani and Nancy Evans thought that I should widen my repertoire and sing lieder. As a result of winning the Purcell–Britten Prize I was given a recital at the Wigmore Hall and I sang Britten's Canticle II: 'Abraham and Isaac' *with Laurence Dale.*

DEREK LEE RAGIN

© Nigel Luckhurst

Heather Harper with James Meek

concert at Blackheath Mansion with Derek Lee Ragin, the American counter-tenor, winner of the Purcell–Britten Prize for Concert Singers and a student at the School; Roderick Shaw (harpsichord), and Julius Drake (piano).

Derek Lee Ragin had been studying at the University of Maryland under Dr James McDonald, who was a close friend of Nancy Evans and Eric Crozier. Visiting McDonald they heard Derek Lee Ragin sing and Nancy said, 'I have never in my life heard a more beautiful counter-tenor. You must come to Snape.' Ragin was studying in Amsterdam when the invitation to Snape came. There was a problem with his entry visa that so infuriated Peter Pears that he actually ended up telephoning the Home Office himself to get the matter settled.

Courses at the School had started that year in March with a Vocal Ensemble course, with Pears, Nancy Evans and Graham Johnson giving masterclasses. The pianists for this course were David Cowan and Jonathan Darlington, now the conductor of the Duisburg Philharmonic Orchestra and Director of the Vancouver Opera.

In April there were a French Song course and a Bach Course. Hugues Cuénod and Gérard Souzay taught the French Song course with Peter Pears and Nancy Evans and the pianists were Iain Burnside, Julius Drake and Adrian Hobbs. Heather Harper joined Pears and Evans for the Bach course with pianists Richard Balcombe, Graham Barber and Ivor Bolton. The instrumentalists were Andrew Roberts and Peter Nall (violins), Peter Collyer (viola), Rachel Maguire (cello), Simon Channing

At the time I was accompanying the masterclasses there was a particularly good crop of – now very well-known – pianists, and as I remember it we were all very good colleagues and enjoyed each others' company: parties were regular events. The overriding memory however of course is of the enormous privilege that one felt simply from being at Aldeburgh. It was, and still is, a sort of mecca for students – both instrumentalists and singers – from all over the world. Peter Pears was the first member of staff whom I encountered, shortly followed by Nancy Evans and Eric Crozier. The list was to extend in a very short time to the likes of Elisabeth Schwarzkopf, Heather Harper, Suzanne Danco and Hugues Cuénod, to name just a few. The amount I learned from them is incalculable and I still think of them in my daily professional life.

The Maltings has a very special atmosphere – the light on the marshes and the intimacy of the surroundings lending it a spiritual aura that seeps into you after a few days and never really leaves you. Everything seems 'exceptional' and for that reason I find it very hard to put my finger on one particular event that stands out from all the rest. Perhaps it would be my first night before my first engagement lying awake in one of the Red Studio beds. Or having to transpose at sight a Hugo Wolf song at one of the concerts. Or the long walks along Aldeburgh beach in the driving wind and rain after fish and chips or . . . or . . . You see once one starts it's hard to stop. Just like Aldeburgh.

JONATHAN DARLINGTON

© Nigel Luckhurst

Eric Crozier in the Faculty Room at the School

© Nigel Luckhurst

Ruggiero Ricci

(flute) and Victoria Trotman (oboe). Among the students were James Meek and Louise Camens, both of whom were to sing in *Owen Wingrave*.

Further courses in 1984 followed the well-established pattern. Course directors included Jan de Gaetani and Ian Partridge in an English and American Song course. Ian Partridge was one of Britain's leading lyric tenors and Jan de Gaetani was a well-known American mezzo-soprano acclaimed for her performance of contemporary music.

Hans Hotter and Kerstin Meyer taught on the German song course. Hans Hotter – the German bass-baritone – had had an operatic career that spanned fifty years; he was considered to be the definitive exponent of some of the great Wagnerian roles, including Wotan and Hans Sachs. He was also a celebrated lieder singer. He was so famous at one time that when once on a visit to London he saw a headline reading 'Hotter in London', it is understandable he did not realize that it referred to the weather. Kerstin Meyer is a distinguished Swedish mezzo-soprano, an opera singer and recitalist and a former member of the Swedish Royal Opera.

Among the students on the German Song course were George Mosley, Gary Coward and Elisabeth Norberg Schultz, a Norwegian who has performed at opera houses all over the world (including at Glyndebourne in 2003). Vishnevskaya returned for a Russian Song course in July, and in August William Pleeth was joined by Ruggiero Ricci, who was invited by Hugh Maguire and whose classes attracted very fine students

Through a wonderful teacher during my early music studies in Australia I was instilled with a dream of singing in Vienna. There is little doubt that my dream would never have come true without the Britten–Pears School.

Over more than one year at the School I had the privilege of singing, studying, living and making friends with distinguished figures, taking part in the masterclasses, being part of two Festival operas and singing the lead in Handel's Rodelinda. *The magnificent homes in which I stayed, the ocean, the reeds and the beauty of the surrounding area was almost a fantasy and I loved and appreciated every moment.*

Firstly, I have never met a famous musician who is not famous for a very good reason – they are simply brilliant at what they do and in Aldeburgh we were surrounded by the best. I remember the breathless shock of hearing Murray Perahia playing for me the introduction of a Mozart aria. I had heard that introduction many times but, as I went to sing, I fell silent – silenced by the beauty of his touch. I remember discussing (and rehearsing) with Iain Burnside the importance of a milli-second pause in the music before a performance, and practising the co-ordination of breath as we began a recital.

I remember Galina Vishnevskaya's magic as she wove imaginary tales around us with her vivid mind's eye. To be part of the world of Sir Peter Pears and his intense love of poetry was stimulating. The help and support of Heather Harper was exactly what I needed. Her strength and agility were exceptional and I adored the opportunity to work on Scandinavian song with Kerstin Meyer and to be in the room working with Hans Hotter. Nancy Evans's exercises and stories were so much a fabulous part of it all and working on language and gaining the friendship of Eric Crozier was a highlight.

It was while I was in Aldeburgh that Sir Peter introduced me to Elisabeth Schwarzkopf and I became the first recipient of the Walter Legge/Elisabeth Schwarzkopf Award and moved to her home in Switzerland. Under the direction of Sir Peter Ustinov and coached by Schwarzkopf, I sang the Countess in a fringe performance of Le nozze di Figaro *at the Salzburg Festival.*

My reward was substantial: a two-year contract at the Vienna State Opera. The training, the confidence-building, the nurturing . . . without the School it never would have happened. I would love to do it all again.

LOUISE CAMENS

© Nigel Luckhurst

Hugues Cuénod

and a large number of observers. It really was an extraordinary coup for the School to engage Ricci to teach at Snape. A legendary violinist, he has had a career covering seventy-five years, starting at the age of ten in 1928. He has given over six thousand concerts all over the world and taught at the finest music colleges in the United States. The pianists for this course were Robert Bridge, Iain Burnside and Peggy Gray. The Prague Quartet was at the School for the Eighth International Academy of String Quartets.

Elisabeth Schwarzkopf was booked for a further series of masterclasses on Mozart in October but due to the flooding of her home in Switzerland, she cancelled the classes the evening before they were due to start. I have no idea whether she ever realized the impact that had or whether she was aware of the level of disappointment felt by the students. At very short notice Ilse Wolf replaced her to join Pears and Evans and this course brought an end to the 1984 School year.

The School staff were to undergo further changes in 1985. Alastair Creamer moved to become the Aldeburgh Foundation's Artists and Concerts Manager and while John Owen continued as the Administrator, he was joined by three new assistants, Mark Kemball, David Mold and Penny Sydenham.

Following the success of the performance of Walton's *Façade* in the 1982 Aldeburgh Festival, it was decided to present a repeat performance in the Drapers' Hall in London in aid of the Aldeburgh Appeal. The performers were again members of the Britten–Pears Orchestra conducted by Hugh Maguire and the speakers were Nancy Evans and Richard Baker. It was a very glamorous occasion and raised a significant sum for the Appeal.

The first course of this year was Bach with Pears, Evans and Heather Harper. There were eleven singers; the accompanists were Ivor Bolton, Iain Burnside and Jonathan Darlington and the instrumentalists were the members of the Brindisi Quartet.

Then came a French Song course with Pears, Evans, Hugues Cuénod and Suzanne Danco. The teaching partnership between Cuénod and Danco was a very happy collaboration and was to continue unbroken for many years. It was one of the best visiting-teacher collaborations that the School was ever able to secure and immensely popular with the students. Cuénod and Danco complemented each other perfectly; she was inclined to be stern and Cuénod was rather more light-hearted. The accompanists for the course were Iain Burnside, Jonathan Darlington and Julius Drake and among the dozen students were Lorna Anderson, James Meek, Nicholas Sears and Stanley Warren.

Nicholas Sears is now the Head of Vocal Studies at the Royal College of Music. He had been a Choral Scholar at Trinity College, Cambridge, and then studied at the Guildhall School. While at the Guildhall he saw an advertisement for courses at the Britten–Pears School, auditioned and was accepted for three of the courses. At the time he was not interested in a career in opera but was attracted to the repertoire being studied at Snape, particularly the German and French song.

Suzanne Danco with a student

At Snape, in those beautiful surroundings, there was time for reflection, for focused, in-depth study of the repertoire in an atmosphere that was dedicated to learning. There was no competitiveness and I know how I valued the opportunity for listening. During a week-long course we listened to all the classes and listened to all our fellow students in a way that was impossible at a conservatoire and this taught us all so much.

In other parts of the world, teachers will come to a particular place for a series of masterclasses; the course takes place and then the teacher leaves – there is no sense whatever of community involvement. This was not the case in Aldeburgh where we felt that we were a part of the town's life.

Snape made me realize exactly what I wanted to do with my career and crystallized my thinking about my future. I loved every moment of the time that I was there.

NICHOLAS SEARS

He was not familiar with the landscape and recalls being struck by the beauty of the reeds and the marshes and the North Sea coastline.

What impressed him most in his first Snape experience was the contrast with the febrile and frantic conservatoire atmosphere. He paid a special tribute to the pianists who 'worked so hard, gave their all, and helped us so much'. He spoke of the international atmosphere at Snape with students from all over the world and the thrill it gave him to be taught by the legendary Hans Hotter and Anna Reynolds and then by Suzanne Danco on the French course.

Like so many students he enjoyed living with an Aldeburgh landlady and said that he particularly noticed that the whole community seemed to be involved with the School activities.

In May the course for the Festival opera, *Rodelinda*, started. Pears and Evans had thought that a Handel opera course (in the composer's tercentenary year) would give the students a particularly valuable learning experience. The conductor was Steuart Bedford and Basil Coleman was the director. Students from the Wimbledon College of Art designed the set. Roger Weaver was the lighting designer and Susan Iles, an Aldeburgh resident who had worked in the wardrobe departments of various London theatres, was the wardrobe mistress.

Philip Shneidman, a resident of New York, was a very remarkable young man. I think that he was probably only about eighteen in 1985 when he wrote to the School asking whether he could stage manage the next opera. He sent his

I think about Aldeburgh all the time – it was a huge influence on my life and, in fact, when starting the Little Opera Theatre, I used what I had learned about the English Opera Group as my model.

And I learned so much there. Basil Coleman was very important in my life. He was always so subtle and he was always correct and clear. He taught me the importance of telling the story of the opera and, of course, it was wonderful to work with someone of Steuart Bedford's experience and knowledge. Steuart always wanted to be involved in every aspect of the production and I remember once seeing him take up a saw and get down to work with it.

I was very foolish as when I arrived I thought, 'Europe. I'll need metric measurements.' So I invested in what I thought was the right equipment only to be met with the carpenter who brought out an antique measure which unfolded and which was, of course, in feet and inches.

When we did Albert Herring *there were some very difficult lighting cues which I consistently got wrong and eventually Steuart told Roger Weaver, who was a talented professional lighting designer living in rural Suffolk, just to ignore whatever I was doing!*

I had a wonderful time at Snape and I cannot overestimate all that I learned from Steuart and Basil.

PHILIP SHNEIDMAN

© Nigel Luckhurst

Director Basil Coleman and conductor Steuart Bedford during rehearsals for Handel's *Rodelinda*

© Nigel Luckhurst

Alison Hagley (Rodelinda) with Edward McGough (Flavio)

CV, which was met with considerable scepticism. 'Surely he cannot possibly have done all the things he says he has done? He is too young.' But he said he was willing to come at his own expense and it was finally decided to give him the chance. As soon as he arrived it became apparent that he had indeed done all the things he said that he had done. He was an unqualified success. Professional to his fingertips, he knew exactly what was needed and was committed and efficient. Everybody liked Philip and he was to return the following year, becoming a popular and essential part of the School opera programme. He now runs the Little Opera Theatre in New York.

The répétiteurs for *Rodelinda* were Richard Balcombe, Nancy Cooley and Stephen Westrop. The two casts were remarkable by any standards.

One of the guards was David Mold, an assistant at the School. As John Owen said, 'If you worked for the School, you might be asked to do anything – including dressing up as a guard and going on stage.'

Rodelinda was a watershed moment in the careers of both Louise Camens and Gerald Finley. Nicholas Clapton, who sang the role of Unolfo, went on to have a successful career in opera, oratorio and recital, and is well known for his performances of contemporary music, having given no fewer than twenty-seven world premieres. He is now a Professor of Singing at the Royal Academy of Music.

Apart from the performances of *Rodelinda*, the Britten–Pears School played a large part in the 1985 Festival. There was a

Handel: Rodelinda
Aldeburgh Festival, 1985

Rodelinda	Louise Camens
	Alison Hagley
Bertarido	Brian Gordon
	Christopher Royal
Grimoaldo	Paul Nilon
	Mark Tucker
Eduige	Margaret Cameron
	Rosalind Eaton
Unulfo	Robert Chavner
	Nicholas Clapton
Garibaldo	Gerald Finley
	Thomas Goerz
Flavio	Edward McGough
The Nurse	Julia Lang

Britten–Pears Orchestra
Leader Patrick Kiernan

Conducted by Steuart Bedford
Directed by Basil Coleman
Lighting Designer Roger Weaver

© Nigel Luckhurst

Louise Camens (Rodelinda) with Edward McGough (Flavio) and Julia Lang (Nurse)

© Nigel Luckhurst

Rodelinda: Brian Gordon (Bertarido) and Paul Nilon (Grimoaldo)

concert on 20 June given by the Britten–Pears Ensemble, a chamber group formed from members of the BPO. Henri Dutilleux, one of the most important French composers of the second half of the twentieth century, was the composer-in-residence. The performers included Tracey Chadwell (soprano), Gerard O'Beirne (tenor), James Meek (baritone), Iain Burnside (piano), Simon Channing (flute), Marios Argiros (oboe), Joy Farrall (clarinet), David Cox (horn), Imogen Barford (harp) and the Brindisi String Quartet.

The Britten–Pears Orchestra, led by Jacqueline Shave, gave a concert conducted by Erich Schmid. The soloists were Imogen Barford, Kari-Lise Ravnan (cello) David Mason (harpsichord) and Iain Burnside. The programme included pieces by Dutilleux, Mozart and Bach, and the *Petite symphonie concertante* by Frank Martin, whose widow visited Aldeburgh and was delighted by the performance.

The Brindisi Quartet gave a late-night concert on 18 June and performed Britten's *Quartettino*. They also took part in a lecture recital, 'The Ondes Martenot', given by Elmer Bernstein and Cynthia Millar. John Owen, who had studied composition at York University and with Richard Rodney Bennett, composed a piece, Quintet, especially for this concert, alongside works by Elmer Bernstein and Richard Rodney Bennett.

The first course after the 1985 Festival was an English and American Song course with Peter Pears, Nancy Evans and Theodor Uppman, the American singer who taken the role of Billy Budd in the first production of Britten's opera. All the

The first memory I have of the Britten–Pears School is the auditions for Rodelinda *in 1985. Having Peter Pears on the panel was quite something – he seemed to look right through you, to know exactly what you were thinking, but also exactly how difficult the whole process might be.*

Then, the weather: we were so lucky with Rodelinda *– weeks of blazing sunshine, as well as the sheer beauty of Snape, the beach at Aldeburgh, the Smugglers' Path; oh, and we had Basil Coleman directing and Steuart Bedford conducting – that certainly helped.*

Sir Peter was also very much about the place: he had recruited Julia Lang to play a non-speaking nurse's role in the opera, and deputed her to teach me how to stand well on stage. She and I had to remain motionless upstage centre for about six minutes at the end of Act II, while Rodelinda and the male-lead Bertarido sang a fabulous duet. Julia told me: 'Just twitch your calf muscles now and then – that way you won't get cramp and nobody notices.'

The next year I was asked back for a St Matthew Passion *in the Maltings, the last course Pears ever taught, and then sang for Hugues Cuénod's and Suzanne Danco's French Song masterclass. Sir Peter, having taught with great vigour and insight on the Bach course that culminated in the performance of the* St Matthew Passion, *died before the course was complete. It was decided by all concerned that 'the show must go on', and it did.*

Cuénod was utterly charming, and very disarming with remarks such as, 'When Poulenc and I used to sing this, we . . .' He was also very 'hot' on text, text, text. Danco I remember as diminutive, politesse incarnate, but capable of real Gallic ferocity as the occasion demanded. Her English (unlike Cuénod's; he was bilingual) was pretty vestigial, so torrents of French were the rule. I loved it all.

Several years later I went back to observe my present teacher Diane Forlano's open masterclass. This woman is a genius, changing people's lives with a few words. I suppose that also sums up the Britten–Pears School: a place that changes lives.

NICHOLAS CLAPTON

© Nigel Luckhurst

William Pleeth

singers on this course were Canadian or American with the exception of Robert Torday. Uppman had a very long and close friendship with both Britten and Pears and was always a good and loyal friend to all those connected with the School and the Festival.

He and his wife, Jean, had a large, comfortable apartment in an old building on the Upper West Side of New York where they welcomed visitors from Aldeburgh with warmth and generosity. They all became familiar with Ted's and Jean's rather eccentric collection of small tortoises.

At the end of July a Scandinavian Song course was held under the direction of Kerstin Meyer, chosen because her extensive knowledge of the repertoire would provide the students with particular insight. Stephen Ralls and Bruce Ubukata were the accompanists. This was followed by a German Song course directed by Hans Hotter and Anna Reynolds. Among the students on this course were Tony Boutté from the United States, Louise Camens and Nicholas Sears.

Galina Vishnevskaya directed her annual Russian Song course with only six specially selected students, including Louise Camens and Hugh Mackey (see pp. 64–5), who was by then a frequent student at Snape.

String Courses began in July with the Ninth International Academy of String Quartets, directed by Hugh Maguire, Patrick Ireland and William Pleeth and with seven student quartets, including the Brindisi Quartet and the Brooks Quartet with Brian Brooks, who frequently led the Britten–

Pears Orchestra. One quartet on the course was from Norway and another from Germany.

This course was followed by the Piano Trio course with Hugh Maguire, William Pleeth and Artur Balsam. Six student trios attended the course, including one, the Esterhazy Quartet, from the United States.

Hugh Maguire and John Owen were delighted that they had been able to persuade Pierre Fournier and Mark Lubotsky, who had recorded Britten's Violin Concerto with the composer conducting, to direct the Solo Violin and Cello masterclasses that followed the Piano Trio course. The accompanists were Michael Dussek and David Tutt. The course attracted students from the United States, Canada, Finland, Germany and Korea, as well Britain.

In September Elisabeth Schwarzkopf returned for one week to give masterclasses with just nine students on the course. She was adamant that she would teach only the very best students and those on the course had been very carefully selected. They included Louise Camens, Nicholas Sears and others from Canada, Australia, Germany and Japan.

The School year ended after this course and it was the conclusion of a very good year. It seemed at the end of 1985, after much trial and error, that a rhythm had been established. The very strict audition process, taking place internationally, was working exactly as the Artistic Directors and John Owen had hoped; the courses were conducted by the finest musicians in the world and the administrative structure of the School was settled. One development was that courses were now of varying length, which was an enormous improvement on the very first years, when they had all been one week long and took place back to back.

In 1986 shattering news was received that affected not only the School and the Aldeburgh community but the musical world as a whole. On 3 April Peter Pears died suddenly following a coronary. The day before his death he had given a remarkable masterclass on the Evangelist role in the Bach Passions, which seemed to everyone there to embody a lifetime's experience, wisdom and understanding. At the end of the session he was talking to the students about the horrors of the Crucifixion and one of them told me that he suddenly smiled and said, 'But then there was the Resurrection.' These were his last words to the students.

Teachers, students and everybody who was connected with the School felt bereft and his death opened a gap that it would be impossible to fill. We all missed his gentle, kindly presence and his humour. But, above all, the School missed his amazing gifts as a teacher, his total commitment to the students as someone who had always done everything possible to encourage them personally and nurture their gifts.

His funeral took place in Aldeburgh Parish Church and he was buried in Aldeburgh churchyard beside Benjamin Britten and Imogen Holst. The day of the funeral was bright and windy. I remember seeing, among all those who were present at the graveside, Murray Perahia, who had flown from New York in Concorde; he was returning immediately afterwards to New York where he had a concert that very same day – a remarkable demonstration of the affection and regard in which Peter Pears was held.

In July a splendid Memorial Service was held in an absolutely packed Westminster Abbey. On 30 November, 'A Tribute to Peter Pears' took place at the Royal Opera House, given in aid of the Aldeburgh Appeal. The first piece was a first performance of a Tribute Fanfare by Colin Matthews, followed by Mozart's *Sinfonia concertante* with soloists Anne-Sophie Mutter (violin) and Bruno Giuranna (viola) and the City of Birmingham Symphony Orchestra conducted by Simon Rattle.

After the interval, there was a performance of Britten's *War Requiem* with the CBSO joined by the Philharmonia Chorus, the choristers of Westminster Cathedral and soloists Galina Vishnevskaya, Anthony Rolfe Johnson and John Shirley-Quirk.

The performance was followed by a reception in the Crush Bar and my enduring memory is of the former prime minister Sir Edward Heath standing with his security officer and, looking typically grumpy, saying, 'It's a rotten piece.'

Everyone knew that Peter Pears would want the School programme to continue uninterrupted and on 7 April the French Song course with Hugues Cuénod and Suzanne Danco started, with Iain Burnside, Nancy Cooley and Martin Martineau as accompanists. Among the students were many who had studied at Snape several times previously, and included Tony Boutté, Louise Camens, Nicholas Clapton and Nicholas Sears. These students, who knew Pears so well and had benefited so much from his teaching, were especially affected by his absence. Looking back now, one realizes that it must have been particularly difficult for Nancy Evans to continue with her teaching and coaching; Peter had been her life-long friend and colleague and she was desolate without him.

In May 1986, rehearsals and classes for the School production of *Albert Herring* began. Steuart Bedford was the conductor, assisted by Stephen Westrop, Basil Coleman the director and Roger Weaver the lighting designer. Sets and design were by the Wimbledon College of Art.

John Owen was the company manager and Philip Shneidman, having made such a good impression in 1985 and because he enjoyed working at Snape, returned from the United States to undertake the stage management. The Britten–Pears Orchestra was led by Jacqueline Shave.

There were four performances, including two matinees, conducted by Stephen Westrop. A discussion led by Eric Crozier, the librettist, was held in the Jubilee Hall and on the panel were members of the original *Albert Herring* cast, including Joan Cross (Lady Billows), Nancy Evans (Nancy), Roy Ashton (Mr Upfold), Catherine Lawson (Mrs Herring in subsequent performances), Norman Lumsden (Superintendant Budd and David Spenser (Harry). Eric Crozier and Nancy Evans also gave a talk entitled 'Albert the Good'.

Britten: Albert Herring
Aldeburgh Festival, 1986

Lady Billows	Halyna Dytniak
	Margaret Maguire
Florence	Kathleen McKellar
	Suzanne Vanstone
Miss Wordsworth	Tracy Bounden
	Tracey Chadwell
Mr Gedge	Mark Monterno
	Mark Wilson
Mr Upfold	Colin McKerracher
	Joseph Zuccata
Superintendant Budd	Alastair Harding
	Christopher Painter
Sid	Roberto Salvatori
	Nathaniel Watson
Albert Herring	Peter Butterfield
	Gerard O'Beirne
Nancy	Sarah Fryer
	Monica Zerbe
Mrs Herring	Marilyn de Blieck
	Jane Mitchell

Albert Herring: May Day in Loxford – a celebration of the virtues of Albert Herring (Gerald O'Beirne)

© Nigel Luckhurst

Murray Perahia rehearsing with the Britten–Pears Orchestra. The front-desk players are Gonzalo Acosta, Lesley Hatfield and Patrick Kiernan.

The Britten–Pears Orchestra, conducted by Hugh Maguire and led by Jacqueline Shave, gave a concert including a Mozart piano concerto with Murray Perahia as the soloist. On Peter Pears's birthday, 22 June, there was a concert given to honour him and to close the Festival. The artists taking part were Steuart Bedford, Murray Perahia, John Shirley-Quirk and Serenata which consisted entirely of players from the Britten–Pears Orchestra including Simon Channing (flute), Mario Argiros (oboe), Janet Hilton (clarinet), Ursula Leveaux (bassoon), David Cox (horn), Jacqueline Shave (violin) Jonathan Barritt (violin), Nicholas Roberts (cello) and Chi-chi Nwanoku (double-bass).

From 7 to 19 July there were Solo Strings masterclasses with Hugh Maguire, Felix Andrievsky, Bruno Giuranna and William Pleeth. The pianists were Iain Burnside, Michael Dussek and Peggy Gray. There were twenty-seven students, including Gonzalo Acosta and Douglas Paterson as well as others from the United States, Canada, Germany, Switzerland and Korea.

In 1983 Mstislav Rostropovich had established a Rostropovich Festival which took place in the Maltings in August of each year. His vision was very wide and he intended it to feature not only music of the very highest standard but also the visual arts with exhibitions of the works of contemporary Russian artists. Rostropovich Festivals took place in 1983, 1984 and 1985, which meant that there was a season of high-quality music outside the Festival itself and that more productive use was made of Snape Maltings Concert Hall.

The first Rostropovich Festival in 1983 included an exhibition of paintings by the contemporary Russian artist, Gabriel Glikman. The exhibition was held in the Recital Room of the School and one of Glikman's works was used for the cover of the Rostropovich Festival programme book. This is a portrait of Mstislav Rostropovich and is remarkable – the body is painted in red and is in the shape of a cello. 'My stomach – cello,' Slava announced with obvious pleasure, in his accented English.

The School was heavily involved in the Rostropovich Festivals. Both Rostropovich and Vishnevskaya gave master-classes and the programme book for the first Festival featured a fine picture of Vishnevskaya teaching a very young Joan Rodgers (see p. 129). Inside the programme book the dedication reads 'Slava and Galina offer this Festival to Ben and Peter with love'. In that 1983 Festival there was a concert given by the Britten– Pears Orchestra, conducted by Rostropovich and led by Brian Brooks, which included a performance of Prokofiev's *Peter and the Wolf*, narrated by Peter Bowring, Chairman of the Aldeburgh Foundation.

The whole Festival was intended to be intimate and personal, a Festival about friends and for friends. Rostropovich and Vishnevskaya hosted a Russian Tea in the Maltings restaurant with Russian tea from a samovar and various Russian jams and sweets.

The second and third Rostropovich Festivals followed the same pattern. In the third Festival Anne-Sophie Mutter, then

© *Nigel Luckhurst*

Mstislav Rostropovich with the Britten–Pears Orchestra at Snape Maltings Concert Hall

Mozart: Così fan tutte
Britten–Mozart Festival, 1986

Fiordiligi	Carmen Pelton
	Susan Waters
Dorabella	Gabrielle Prata
	Rachael Hallawell
Ferrando	Benoit Boutet
	Cristian Carrasco
Guglielmo	Gerald Finley
	George Mosley
Don Alfonso	Alastair Harding
	Mark Moliterno
Despina	Sung Ha Shin
	Zoe Hwang

Britten–Pears Orchestra
Leader Gonzalo Acosta

Musical Direction by Murray Perahia and Ivor Bolton
Directed by Basil Coleman
Vocal Coach Thomas Hemsley

just into her twenties, was the featured violinist performing the Tchaikovsky Violin Concerto with the Philharmonia Orchestra. Mutter and Rostropovich were joined by Bruno Giuranna in an unforgettable programme of Beethoven string trios.

After the 1985 Rostropovich Festival, there were planning discussions for 1986. Rostropovich announced that as part of his Festival, he wanted to invite every Russian dissident to come to Snape and, somewhat bizarrely, to meet on the banks of the River Alde. This obviously required approval from the Council of the Aldeburgh Foundation but they vetoed the plan, on the grounds that it was too political. Rostropovich interpreted this as a slight and as craven behaviour and decided that there would be no further Rostropovich Festivals.

This decision meant that there was a gap in the plans to present a summer season of music in the Concert Hall and as a result the ideas of extending the Proms throughout August and a series of concerts in September linking the works of Britten with those of another composer was mooted. In 1986 the other composer chosen for the Britten Festival was Mozart and as a consequence the School began work on *Così fan tutte.*

This opera course was an enormously important step in the development of the School and saw its work effectively taken up a further notch. It was a much more ambitious undertaking than anything the School had previously attempted. Murray Perahia was to direct the course, assisted by Ivor Bolton. The producer was Basil Coleman and the vocal coach was Thomas Hemsley. Roger Andrews was the designer and the répétiteurs

© Nigel Luckhurst

Così fan tutte: Gabrielle Prata (Dorabella) and Carmen Pelton (Fiordiligi)

© Nigel Luckhurst

Così fan tutte: Fiordiligi and Dorabella (Carmen Pelton and Gabrielle Prata) are wooed by two strangely familiar Albanians (Benoit Boutet and Gerald Finley)

Nancy Cooley and Jonathan Dove, who was later to become a composer, most notably of opera.

Murray Perahia had been present at the first masterclasses in 1972 and was very familiar with the School and with the Festival; he became one of the Artistic Directors of the Festival in 1983. He remembers Pears talking to him about the School's development at the time of the building. He told me that the *Così fan tutte* course had been Peter's idea which, of course, gave the whole project an added poignancy.

Perahia said that the course was wonderful because it was given so much time. For the students, working with an artist of Murray Perahia's distinction, over a long period, was an extraordinary opportunity and one that they could probably have had nowhere else. They valued every moment of the time spent on the course and still talk of the insights and subtleties of the music that Perahia's direction gave them.

An 'Opera Forum', chaired by Sir Denis Forman, was held before the first performance. Dr Stanley Sadie, Murray Perahia, Basil Coleman and Thomas Hemsley were members of the panel. Sir Denis Forman, author of *The Good Opera Guide* and Chairman of Granada Television, himself a very good amateur pianist, was a friend of Perahia. The discussion was lively and informative and apart from the musical discussion, it gave the audience insights into the darker complexities of the opera.

There were four performances, two sponsored – one, somewhat surprisingly, by Birds Eye Walls. The company had a factory in Lowestoft where one might have expected them to manufacture fish fingers but this was where beefburgers were produced. The manager responsible for these beefburgers was a lover of classical music and persuaded his colleagues to support one performance of *Così fan tutte*.

The other sponsor was Brian Taylor, a Suffolk opera-lover, who had made a fortune when his Manningtree company, which manufactured plastics and safety equipment, went public. He became a stalwart supporter of the School and all its activities. Commercial sponsorship of the School was developing well at this time and we were gaining support from new, and sometimes unlikely, sources.

When Murray Perahia made the decision, at the last moment, to hand over to Ivor Bolton the conducting of the actual performances, in spite of a natural disappointment everyone remarked on Perahia's extraordinary modesty and professionalism. Shortly afterwards Ivor Bolton became chorus-master at Glyndebourne and is now the Chief Conductor of the Mozarteum Orchestra Salzburg and works regularly in Munich, Paris, at the Royal Opera House and at Glyndebourne.

Before work on the opera started there had been lengthy discussions about making a documentary for television highlighting the work of the School in the context of all the other musical activities at Aldeburgh. Michael Darlow agreed to direct the film and it was decided that it would be focused on the *Così fan tutte* course. In the event the film, *The Aldeburgh Story*, was made and shown on Channel 4 as a three-part series.

It was such fun, and one of the things that made it such fun was that the singers seemed to become their characters. It's lovely, because I still see some of the singers when I am abroad. I've seen Zoe Hwang and Carmen Pelton and Benoit Boutet; they come to my concerts and then come back to see me, so I've kept in touch with them.

It was all amazing and the kids were just wonderful. I did all the rehearsals – all the piano rehearsals and even the dress rehearsal but at the last moment I pulled out. I was just too scared . . . the recitatives . . . and I handed over to Ivor Bolton who did very well. It was all so exciting and I shall never forget the first performance which was wonderful, fabulous. They were all so young – the singers and the orchestra. It was such a big development for the School. I have a photograph which I treasure of Basil holding my son Ben, who was a baby, watching me conducting.

MURRAY PERAHIA

Continued on page 183

I worked at the Britten–Pears School three times in 1986–87. The first experience was extraordinary. I was répétiteur for Così fan tutte, *rehearsed by Murray Perahia, although eventually the performances were conducted by Ivor Bolton. I had come directly from working in Italy, and hadn't found time to practise the score. I was horrified to find myself sight-reading Mozart in front of perhaps the most famous Mozart pianist of our day. In fact, he was very forgiving, although he was puzzled when – turning pages for another pianist – I added an extra bass note to my favourite phrase in the Act I finale (it was this phrase that got me hooked on Mozart's operas). Over coffee, he said, 'I notice you added some octave doubling.' I replied, casually, 'Oh, just for fun.' The temperature seemed to drop, and I felt I had uttered some blasphemy as he stared at me and said, slowly, 'Oh. I see. For fun.'*

But it seemed that just being near him made us all excel ourselves: his vision of the piece and his demonstration of significant passages were so inspiring that something seemed to rub off. On one occasion, one of the singers overheard me playing in the Concert Hall and thought it was Murray Perahia! (That has never happened again.) I was amazed by the way he inhabited the music. There was never any empty passagework; never a semi-quaver that wasn't part of a phrase, coming from somewhere and going somewhere else. It was wonderfully energizing, so completely alive. When he went to the piano to show how he was hoping the tenors would sing 'Un'aura amorosa', the expressive legato line he could conjure from a percussion instrument was simply astonishing.

Sometimes he struggled to get the singers to understand the nuances of tempo and phrasing he was hoping for. 'And here, I just want you to love it a little,' he said. 'You mean you want a ritard in bar 6?' asked an efficient American soprano.

The music seemed to speak to him so directly, it was as if he had fewer layers of skin than the rest of us. I noticed a sense of disappointment when we were rehearsing 'Soave sia il vento' – there was something missing, and he didn't know how to get it. I realized that he couldn't achieve a 'magical' arrival on a particular chord because everyone was breathing at that point. I suggested they breathe earlier – the magic happened – and the most beautiful smile lit up his face. I was thrilled to have been able to help this extraordinary musician release that moment of wonder.

Feeling that we had such a valuable person in our midst, it made me nervous to be driven down the narrow country lanes with him at breakneck speed by Ivor Bolton, who always claimed to be 'fast, but safe'. I felt we had a responsibility to protect our precious cargo, but Murray didn't seem in the least perturbed, and talked about the discoveries he had made in Schenkerian analyses of many of the arias, as we headed towards the Butley Orford Oysterage. I have never known a conductor prepare an opera in this way. It was fascinating, and made me want to raise my own game.

The remote location of the Maltings created a sense of calm and focus, and being surrounded by so many enthusiastic young artists in a place with such an important tradition was conducive to creativity. That first summer, I was trying to finish a piano duet in my spare time, and loved the feeling that I was working at a piano where Britten might have composed, looking out at the view he would have seen. It wasn't inhibiting; it was encouraging. There was a sense that great things were possible.

The lonely beauty of the fens was particularly appealing to one of the singers the following year: Simon Keenlyside, who was singing Tarquinius in The Rape of Lucretia, *was a keen birdwatcher and often came to rehearsals with tales of rare birds he'd spotted that morning. The conductor was Steuart Bedford, who had worked a great deal with Britten, as had the director, Basil Coleman. This sense of immediate connection with the great genius of British music was a great part of the excitement of being at the Maltings.*

If occasionally the atmosphere seemed so polite that it made one want to rebel, perhaps that was no bad thing. It provoked vitality. And it still moves me to think of the composer whose wide-ranging creative and practical gifts equipped him, with his partner, to start a festival and a school that would enrich our musical life for so long.

JONATHAN DOVE

Jonathan Dove

© Ben Wright Photography

Ivor Bolton

My first professional work was at Snape when I played for Bach masterclasses. It was an idyllic place and I enjoyed everything about it, particularly the colleagues with whom I worked there. I remember especially how much pleasure I got from the daily routine – the private coaching and the public masterclasses in the afternoon. There was a rhythm to life, very long hours of hard work and then relaxing with friends in the evenings – probably in the pub.

Working with Murray Perahia was an inspiration. He had such musical insight and a mind of great originality. He was a perfectionist and he had amazingly high standards. He understood so clearly the long-range structure of the music and the harmonic underpinning of that structure, things that we had all studied but which he incarnated. His decision to entrust me with conducting the performances was evidence of his humility and his determination to deliver his own high standards.

After the dress rehearsal with the first cast and the debriefing afterwards, conducted by Murray, we had a rehearsal of the overture with the orchestra in which he was able to concentrate entirely on the orchestra. He worked so hard and with such enthusiasm.

Aldeburgh helped me to decide on my future career and to focus on working with singers. I returned many times and it became like an island in my life.

Ivor Bolton

During the year there were two further Singers courses, a Russian Song course with Galina Vishnevskaya and a Britten course. The Tenth International Academy of String Quartets brought the School year to an end.

The School had now been established in its own home for eight years and the annual programme had fallen into a regular pattern, with constant small adjustments that improved the effectiveness of individual courses. Nicholas Winter joined the School staff as an assistant to John Owen. Nick, now the Artistic Administrator of the Chicago Symphony Orchestra, is extremely accomplished and an outstanding linguist with perfect Russian as well as being fluent in a number of other languages. He made a valuable contribution to the running of the School and subsequently to the Foundation as a whole when later he – as had so many previous assistants at the School – took on another role. John Owen continued to administer the School with flair and efficiency.

The first course of 1987 was a Bach course directed by Nancy Evans, Heather Harper and John Shirley-Quirk, with accompanists Neil Beardmore, Jonathan Dove and Catherine Edwards. This was followed by a French Song course directed by Hugues Cuénod, Suzanne Danco and Jana Papandopulo with accompanists Nancy Cooley, Jonathan Darlington and Martin Martineau. Jana Papandopulo invariably accompanied Danco and Cuénod when they came to Snape where her advice to the students was always appreciated. Born in Bulgaria,

Britten: The Rape of Lucretia
Aldeburgh Festival, 1987

Male Chorus	Salvatore Champagne
	Michael Powell
Female Chorus	Hope Hudson
	Adrianne Pieczonka
Lucretia	Anne McWatt
	Barbara Rearick
Lucia	Mary Aston
	Meinir Williams
Bianca	Sandra Porter
	Norma Ritchie
Tarquinius	Joseph Corbett
	Simon Keenlyside
Junius	Andrew Greenan
	James Ottaway
Collatinus	Alan Ewing
	Brian Matthews

The Britten–Pears Orchestra
Leader Gonzalo Acosta
Conducted by Steuart Bedford
Directed by Basil Coleman
Designed by Roger Andrews

© Nigel Luckhurst

Simon Keenlyside (Tarquinius) and Anne McWatt (Lucretia)

We all had an amazing time. I especially loved working with Basil Coleman who was absolutely wonderful. We all adored him. He really was a working man and loved working with young people to whom he gave a remarkably free rein. We learned a huge amount from Steuart Bedford and I remember that Reginald Goodall came to one of the rehearsals and talked to us about our work. Nancy Evans was a marvellous coach and so was Bryan Drake [who had created roles in Britten's Curlew River *and* The Burning Fiery Furnace*]. Bryan said to me, 'Well, all things being equal, there is no reason why you shouldn't have a career.' There was such a special atmosphere at Snape and it fired me up and made me certain about what I wanted to do.*

SIMON KEENLYSIDE

Papandopulo was married to the Croatian composer Boris Papandopulo and had herself had a successful career as a singer in Croatia.

In May rehearsals for *The Rape of Lucretia* started. The director was Basil Coleman and the conductor Steuart Bedford. Stephen Westrop was the assistant conductor, Roger Andrews the designer and Bryan Drake the vocal coach. The répétiteurs were Jonathan Dove and Steven Naylor. The Britten–Pears Orchestra was led by Gonzalo Acosta.

The Rape of Lucretia opened the 1987 Aldeburgh Festival and was very enthusiastically received. There were four performances during the Festival.

For Simon Keenlyside this was his first experience of Aldeburgh but he already knew a great deal about it as his grandfather was Leonard Hirsch, the founder of the Hirsch Quartet, and a friend of Britten. His father, Raymond Keenlyside, was a member of the Aeolian Quartet; he had performed at the Festival and while he was there he made several sketches of the beach at Aldeburgh; so for Simon it was familiar territory. In 1987 Keenlyside was studying at the Royal Northern College of Music when the opportunity to sing in *The Rape of Lucretia* arose.

That same year Simon Keenlyside made his professional debut at the Hamburg State Opera singing Count Almaviva in *Le nozze di Figaro* and a very distinguished career has followed. In 1995 Simon was awarded both the Critics Circle and the Royal Philhamonic Society Singer of the Year Award. In 2005

© *Nigel Luckhurst*

Barbara Rearick (Lucretia) and Joseph Corbett (Tarquinius)

I was studying at the Manhattan School of Music and was persuaded to audition for the role of Lucretia. I completely fell in love with the music and it was such a thrill to be selected for the part. Being in England and at Snape was so much more wonderful than I could possibly have imagined and it was such a privilege to work with Steuart Bedford and Nancy Evans and Basil Coleman; one felt a direct link to the composer. I suppose one of the things that I most remember was their encouragement and the way they helped one to to do the very best one could. And I remember, too, the friendships formed. Steuart seemed to me to be an essentially shy man but we would all meet for drinks in the Cross Keys and sit around debating and talking about the music we had been rehearsing and he became so open and helpful. Of course, it was at Snape that I met John Owen who has become my agent and to whom, I feel I owe everything.

Barbara Rearick

his performance in the title role of *Billy Budd* in the ENO production was well received and he says how glad he was to have the opportunity to see Ted Uppman, the original Billy Budd, and to have the chance to discuss the role with him.

The American mezzo-soprano Barbara Rearick, who sang Lucretia, became a firm favourite with teachers and staff at the School and gave the first performance of Colin Matthews's orchestral arrangement of Britten's *A Charm of Lullabies* at the Festival. The original work was written for Nancy Evans and it was she who selected Barbara Rearick for this important occasion. Rearick was also a member of the Britten–Pears Ensemble, a group that John Owen founded in order to explore the wealth of repertoire for voice and ensemble. Barbara Rearick is now one of the most sought-after interpreters of Britten's music in the USA.

Adrianne Pieczonka, a Canadian who was originally funded by the Canadian Aldeburgh Foundation, has become a leading soprano and has performed at all the world's major opera houses. She sang with Plácido Domingo in *Simon Boccanegra* at the Metropolitan Opera and in *Arabella* at the Vienna State Opera. She made her Bayreuth debut some years ago and, apart from the great European opera houses, she has sung in San Francisco, Los Angeles, Houston and, of course, New York. Adrianne Pieczonka and Simon Keenlyside met at Snape and have remained good friends and colleagues.

The School played a prominent part in this Festival. Apart from the four performances of *The Rape of Lucretia*, the closing

I attended the Britten–Pears School in 1987, I believe it was May and June. The opera that year was The Rape of Lucretia *and it was directed by Basil Coleman, a long-time collaborator of Ben's and Peter's and now a dear old friend. (I moved to London in 1995 and lived near Basil for over ten years.) He is now over ninety years old and still going strong! Steuart Bedford conducted the opera. It was an absolute treat and an honour to work with such renowned Britten specialists.*

There were several singers who lodged in flats in houses in the village of Aldeburgh but I and I think about six or seven other singers shared an amazing old house in the tiny village of Thorpeness, about a mile north of Aldeburgh, right on the North Sea.

One of my roommates in Thorpeness was the now famous baritone Simon Keenlyside. He sang the role of Tarquinius and I sang the role of Female Chorus. Simon was an avid bird-watcher and he'd go out to track birdsong at about four in the morning. Quite an eccentric Englishman!

I believe we were a veritable United Nations in the house: Canada, England, Wales, Scotland, New Zealand were all represented. The house was filled with laughter and music: we would eat our breakfast together, huddled in the sitting room of the huge house, eating toast and Marmite (I'd never tried this before!) and we would often put on Britten's Sea Interludes *as we gazed out at the chilly North Sea, the subject of his composition.*

I will never forget the experience at the Britten–Pears School. It was a huge opportunity for me to sing this challenging role at a relatively young age but there were excellent pianists and vocal coaches who encouraged and guided us.

I think mostly I will remember the 'Englishness' of it all: coming from Toronto, it was indeed a culture shock, drinking a pint of Suffolk ale in a tiny pub in Snape. The thick Suffolk accent was quite hard to understand at first and we all did our best to imitate it. I made friends with whom I am still in contact and it sealed for me a love of England and all things English, and most definitely a love of Britten's music.

ADRIANNE PIECZONKA

Franco Gulli

concert of the Festival was given by the Britten–Pears Orchestra, led by Caroline Balding, and there was a further performance of *Façade*. On 22 June – always marked as Peter Pears's birthday – there was a concert in which a chamber ensemble, led by Jacqueline Shave, gave a first performance of a work by John Hopkins.

In July the Solo String course was held, directed by Franco Gulli, Daniel Benyamini and William Pleeth. Daniel Benyamini had previously taught on the String Quartet course as a member of the Tel Aviv Quartet and this was the first course on which Franco Gulli taught. Franco Gulli has been described as one of the most important artists of the twentieth century and was an international soloist and prize-winner. He was to return to the School to teach and became a revered faculty member. There were twenty-seven students on the course, including Koreans, Canadians, Americans, Norwegians and Germans.

As Nicholas Sears remarked of the Singers courses, this international dimension was of great benefit to the students, allowing them to observe the context in which they were hoping to make careers.

The Solo Strings course was followed by the Eleventh International String Quartet Academy, directed by Patrick Ireland, William Pleeth and Kyung-Wha Chung, who was a guest teacher. There were six quartets on this course, in. cluding the Acosta Quartet led by Gonzalo Acosta.

In August Galina Vishnevskaya returned for the Russian Song course. The accompanists were Stephen Ralls and Bruce

Ubukata, and Dmitri Makaroff, a priest in the Russian Orthodox Church, was once again the language coach. There were seven students on the course, including Carl Halvorson from the United States and Coleen Gaetano, the daughter of friends of the Rostropovich family in the US and a protégée of Galina Vishnevskaya.

Hans Hotter was booked to return to Snape for the German Song course at the end of August but in the event ill-health prevented him from coming and his place was taken by Kurt Equiluz, a man John Owen regards as one of the best teachers ever to come to the School and for whom he retains tremendous admiration. The accompanists on this course were Stephen Ralls and Bruce Ubukata.

German song was followed by a Britten course, directed by Anthony Rolfe Johnson and Heather Harper, both of whom were regular teachers at the School and Directors of the Vocal courses.

September saw the start of rehearsals for the out-of-Festival School opera. French music was at the heart of this mini-festival and the selected opera was Debussy's *Pelléas et Mélisande.* The director was Suzanne Danco, herself a famous Mélisande, and the opera was conducted by Steuart Bedford. The répétiteurs were Iain Burnside, Nancy Cooley and Jonathan Darlington.

There were tremendous difficulties over this project. A meeting between Donald Mitchell, Marion Thorpe, the Artistic Directors and John Owen was held. Both Donald Mitchell and

© *Arno Drucker*

Kurt Equiluz

> *The most remarkable thing about Kurt Equiluz was that he spoke very little English and it didn't matter at all. He made his ideas and thoughts so absolutely clear to the students that the fact that he spoke only in German was irrelevant.*
>
> John Owen

Debussy: Pelléas et Mélisande
French Music Festival, 1987

Pelléas	Erik Oland
	Nicholas Sears
Mélisande	Juliet Booth
	Helen Fehily
Golaud	John Davies
	Andrew Greenan
Geneviève	Louise van Winkle
Arkel	Brian Bannatyne-Scott
	Brian Matthews
Yniold	Sandra Lisenden
	Tosi Poleri

Britten–Pears Orchestra
Conducted by Steuart Bedford
Directed by Suzanne Danco

Marion Thorpe were concerned about the choice of *Pelléas et Mélisande*, which they thought would not have box-office appeal or fully engage its audience. Their view was that although Debussy's opera might be considered a masterpiece by some, it still had its longueurs in performance. John Owen remembers Steuart Bedford taking the opposite view and arguing for the virtues of the opera, both for the students on the course and for their audience, and the whole discussion becoming animated and fairly tense.

In the event, reluctant permission to go ahead was given but only on the condition that there were not two performances of the opera. There was to be one performance of Acts I, II, and III, followed the next day by a repeat of Act III, followed by Acts IV and V. John Owen still views this as an 'absolutely ridiculous' decision.

The first performance of *Pelléas et Mélisande* was scheduled for 16 October but on the night of 15–16 October 1987 the great hurricane struck southern England and Suffolk was one of the counties most badly hit by the storm. John Owen describes the destruction: 'So many trees were blown down and the borrowed Jaguar narrowly missed being hit – a tree on either side of it came down but the Jaguar was unscathed. Poor Nancy Cooley's car was hit and absolutely flattened. It looked as though a giant had stepped on it.'

Hugues Cuénod, eighty-four years old at the time, was in Aldeburgh. He surveyed the devastation and remarked with heartfelt compassion, 'I feel so sorry for the peasants.'

There was no electric power at the Maltings. Everything there was pitch dark but Steuart Bedford remembers that it was just possible to hold an afternoon rehearsal in the Concert Hall restaurant as sufficient daylight came through the very large windows. But urgent action needed to be taken and with enormous speed and lightning-fast negotiations, arrangements were made for the first performance – Acts I, II and III – to take place that night in the sports hall of Woodbridge School. Bob Ling organized the workers and everything was transported to Woodbridge where the first performance took place to great acclaim, although, as John Owen says, 'The acoustics were awful.'

Miraculously power was restored the next day and the performance of Acts III, IV and V could take place in Snape Maltings Concert Hall on 17 October. Despite its shaky beginnings and despite being caught up in the great 1987 hurricane, the opera played to enthusiastic audiences and was generally considered to have been a success.

Pelléas et Mélisande was the last course in 1987 and ended the School year. It was also the year in which I left Aldeburgh to work in London at the Barbican Centre.

Alistair Creamer, Moira Bennett and Kenneth Baird

Continuity and Continuation 1987–91

By 1988 the Britten–Pears School had settled into its regular calendar of courses, sixteen years after the first masterclasses. The Directors and the administrative staff were now confident that they knew what worked, what was most successful and what offered the greatest opportunities for the students. The School felt settled and assured of the way ahead.

The audition process for which John Owen was largely responsible had been tried and tested; auditions were held regularly in a number of locations in the United States and Canada, as well as in the United Kingdom and mainland Europe. Although recordings were still used on occasion – and the advent of videotape had made the whole process more reliable – most students could be auditioned in person. Video recordings proved helpful when casting operas. The audition system ran on well-oiled wheels and ensured that the highest standards in the selection of students were maintained. A glance at the lists of participating students reflects the determination of the Director and staff to make sure that the School offered places only to those who would gain the greatest benefit from attending courses.

Further evidence of the School's success was the nucleus of fine teachers returning to lead courses year after year. Suzanne Danco, Ileana Cotrubas and Galina Vishnevskaya were still at this period giving masterclasses nowhere else in the world. They came to Snape because they knew that they would be working with highly talented students and, perhaps, because they so much enjoyed their time at the School.

Moira Bennett, during a fundraising trip to New York, takes coffee with Theodor Uppman.

Peter Pears had always invited guest teachers to a dinner party at the Red House during their visit; after his death this tradition was maintained by Rita Thomson, the senior nurse who had remained at the Red House after supporting first Britten and later Pears. She was a lively, thoughtful and sensitive hostess. Her dinner parties were popular with the visiting teachers, not only adding to their pleasure but making them feel welcome and fully involved in Aldeburgh's work.

Undoubtedly one of the reasons that they enjoyed the Snape experience was the personal care they received from John Owen. There was no question of any of the visiting teachers being met at the airport by a taxi sent by a staff member; Owen always went to the airport himself, met them and drove them to Suffolk. During courses they were never just left to their own devices; unless they preferred to be on their own, Owen would always join them for dinner. He showed enormous respect for these world-famous musical luminaries and he thought that they should be treated as honoured guests rather than simply as contracted teachers. Naturally, they responded well to this treatment and appreciated his care.

His attitude also helped ensure that they would choose to return. Many had travelled a great distance and were happy to spend a week, ten days or perhaps a longer period in a fairly isolated part of the Suffolk coast. Owen saw to it that they never felt that they were strangers in an unfamiliar environment and that a real atmosphere of friendship and something approaching family unity developed.

There was a shared ambition for the School. The Directors and staff were at one in their aspirations and, as so many of the teachers were not strangers but regular visitors who felt at home in Aldeburgh and Snape, they too came to share the same hopes and expectations. The visiting teachers often stayed in local hotels in Aldeburgh but several of them chose to have a bed-and-breakfast arrangement with an Aldeburgh landlady and lasting friendships were formed as a consequence.

Pamela Embleton is the owner of a beautiful house in Aldeburgh, which annually became a home from home for Suzanne Danco, Jana Papandopulo and Hugues Cuénod, who grew to be her close friends. Until recently, Hugues Cuénod was the only survivor of the trio; Pam Embleton visited him regularly in Switzerland until his death in 2010.

The first course of 1988 was the French Song course with teachers Hugues Cuénod and Suzanne Danco, and vocal coach Jana Papandopulo. This course had become an annual feature of the School year. Suzanne Danco, ever elegant and sophisticated, was a demanding teacher always expecting much of her students, who all had a very high regard for her. The eighty-six-year-old Hugues Cuénod was a legendary figure and the students were particularly keen to study with him and gain the benefit of his vast experience. His charm and lightness of touch ensured that he was also greatly loved.

The next course was a Mahler and Berg course directed by Heather Harper, John Shirley-Quirk and Martin Isepp, all three steeped in this repertoire. Both singers had performed Mahler with the world's great Mahler conductors and orchestras. Shirley-Quirk had sung *Kindertotenlieder* with Britten, and Harper had recorded Berg with Pierre Boulez. Isepp's mother, Helene, was a singing teacher, a refugee from Nazi Germany.

The School opera scheduled for performance in the Festival was Tchaikovsky's *Iolanta*. It was directed by Galina Vishnevskaya, conducted by Steuart Bedford and Bryan Drake was the voice consultant. The designer was David Tindle and the répétiteurs were Stephen Ralls and Bruce Ubukata.

The idea of inviting an artist of David Tindle's calibre to design the set was a brilliant one, especially as this Royal Academician had at an early stage in his career been a scenery painter; he painted the *Iolanta* set himself on the paint frame at Warwick Arts Centre.

Vishnevskaya had her own ideas – as she had had over the *Eugene Onegin* set when she had vetoed one by one the ideas submitted by the designer. John Owen travelled to Paris to show Tindle's drawings to Vishnevskaya but each time she would reject the ideas with an uncompromising 'No.'

Finally a very beautiful design of an enclosed, almost secret, garden received her approval but she did not realize that the opening into the enclosed garden was too small for the supernumaries to leave the stage in reasonable time. When this problem emerged in rehearsal she announced, 'It has to be changed by the ten o'clock rehearsal tomorrow morning.'

Owen telephoned David Tindle, expecting him to be considerably irritated but in fact he was sanguine. He suggested

John Shirley-Quirk giving an English Song masterclass in 1980. The accompanist is Roger Vignoles.

Tchaikovsky: Iolanta Aldeburgh Festival, 1988	
Iolanta	Coleen Gaetano
	Jane Webster
René, King of Provence	Michael Druiett
	Keith Kibbler
Count Vaudémont	David Davenport
	Lars Pelarius
Ibn-Hakia	John Hancock
	Julian Long
Robert, Duke of Burgundy	John Davies
	Arkady Volodus
Alméric	David Anderson
Bertrand	Nigel Williams
Martha	Hilary Brooks
	Lisa Monheit
Brigitta	Susan Rosenbaum
	Barbara Walsh
Laura	Sarah Fryer
	Charlotte Hellekant

Britten–Pears Orchestra
Leader Kathryn Greely
Conducted by Steuart Bedford
Directed by Galina Vishnevskaya
Sets designed by David Tindle

ways in which the set could be adapted but as Owen did not feel confident to see them through himself, Tindle nobly agreed to come to Aldeburgh and take charge of the changes. A car was sent that night from Saxmundham to Leamington Spa to bring Tindle back to Aldeburgh, where the artist slept for two hours. In the morning he went out to the Maltings to make the alterations in time for the rehearsal. Owen describes the whole episode as 'a nightmare. It was one of the most stressful times of my life.'

The two Iolantas were very different sizes and shapes, but Vishnevskaya insisted that they wear the same borrowed costume. This resulted in poor Sue Iles, the wardrobe mistress, sitting backstage and frantically either taking the costume in or letting it out.

There were two tenors singing Count Vaudémont. Lars Pelarius was marvellous in the role and David Davenport was also a very good singer, but at the time he was unwell and his illness caused him problems when walking. Lars Pelarius sang in the first performance, to great acclaim, and then, for no reason that anyone could fathom at the time, or understands to this day, he simply walked away, got himself to an airport and was not heard of again.

In the second performance David Davenport sang the role, but hobbling about the stage did nothing for his image as the romantic lead and the fact that Vishnevskaya had forced him to wear an unsuitable blond wig only added to his problems. 'It was an absolute farce,' John Owen says. 'I sat there cringing.'

Donald Mitchell and Marion Thorpe, Trustees of the Britten–Pears Foundation and members of the Education Policy Committee, had been against the choice of *Pelléas et Mélisande* as a School opera in 1987, even though it had not formed part of the Festival. For some time they had been expressing doubts about School opera productions being of a sufficiently high standard for inclusion in the Festival itself and these concerns were now, after the *Iolanta* performances, being aired once more.

School opera productions – in which the performers, however gifted and well prepared, were inexperienced young singers at the start of their careers – could not be compared to stagings by professional opera companies, with all their resources. The opera courses, like everything else at the School at that time, operated on a shoe-string budget and both the staff and the Directors were always working to achieve the highest standards possible in difficult circumstances with begged and borrowed costumes, borrowed or makeshift sets, everything done on the cheap. Given these limitations, what had been achieved was truly remarkable.

It should be remembered that the original reason for School opera productions becoming a part of the Aldeburgh Festival was the result of the dire financial situation in which the Foundation found itself in 1983. It had not been able to afford to engage a professional company and the standards set by the School in response to this challenge were as high as could be managed within the inevitable constraints.

The decision of the Education Committee that School operas would no longer form a part of the June Festival was a blow to both the School administration and to the Directors and it caused considerable dissension. However, the Britten–Pears Foundation was the main funder of the School and the views of the Trustees, who were, at the same time, members of the Education Policy Committee, carried great weight.

Had Peter Pears, such a passionate champion of the School, still been alive, it is possible that the outcome might have been different but, in the circumstances, *Iolanta* proved to be the final nail in the coffin for School opera productions as part of the Aldeburgh Festival. From then on, while staged School productions continued to take place on the Maltings stage, they were not part of the Festival.

There remained a Britten–Pears Orchestra concert in the Festival and both students and former students continued to appear in concerts and recitals. In 1988, Anna Steiger sang Britten's *Les Illuminations* with Sir Neville Marriner conducting the BPO. There was also an Aldeburgh Connection concert, featuring Jane Leslie MacKenzie, Catherine Robbin, Gerald Finley and Peter Butterfield, presented by Stephen Ralls and Bruce Ubukata. The Brindisi Quartet performed in a Britten and Berg concert and Gerald Finley and Nicholas Sears took part in a concert celebrating the music of Francis Poulenc.

In July the regular String courses took place: Solo Viola with Nobuko Imai and the Twelfth International String Quartet Academy with Hugh Maguire, Patrick Ireland and William

© Richard Hubert Smith

Ileana Cotrubas working with a student during the 1988 Mozart course. The pianist is Malcolm Martineau.

Pleeth. This was followed by the Franco Gulli masterclasses. The last String course in 1988 was for Solo Cello, directed by William Pleeth.

In July Ileana Cotrubas came to Snape to direct a Mozart course with Nancy Cooley, Malcolm Martineau and Jonathan Darlington as accompanists. Cotrubas, a native of Romania, was known to British audiences through appearances first at Glyndebourne and then at the Royal Opera; she had sung with the Vienna State Opera, the Metropolitan Opera and in all the greatest international opera houses. This was the first year that she had given masterclasses at Snape and there were applications from students from all over the world. She returned to the School regularly and while she was highly regarded, her outspoken manner caused some distress among the students. This led to misunderstandings and her eventual decision to leave. Her relationship with John Owen was warm and they remained on good terms throughout.

The Cotrubas classes were followed by a Voice and Piano Duo course led by Martin Isepp and Ralf Gothóni. Although a similar course focusing on the equal relationship between singer and pianist had taken place much earlier, it had not been programmed again until now. It was to prove to be so popular with the students that it was re-established as an occasional course. In all other School courses the pianist's role was to accompany the singers or instrumentalists. There were nine duos attending. Malcolm Martineau accompanied two of the singers who came to the course as individuals without established duo partnerships. All the other student duos were already accustomed to working together.

The 1988 School year ended with a German Song course directed by Kurt Equiluz and a course on Britten and His Contemporaries directed by Heather Harper and Anthony Rolfe Johnson.

Kenneth Baird officially left the Aldeburgh Foundation in November 1988 in order to take up the position of Music Director of the Arts Council of Great Britain but he retained – with formal approval – his Aldeburgh responsibilities until Sheila Colvin took over as his successor in the spring of 1989. Colvin was an experienced arts administrator who had been at the Edinburgh Festival for many years. When she arrived she found that the School was being run very effectively.

While the School Directors and John Owen always aimed to think of new themes and new and exciting directors for the courses, the years were now more or less following a familiar pattern. In the beginning much time had, of necessity, been taken up with trying to establish routines for the students and trying to solve the inevitable problems connected with student life – accommodation, catering and transport. All these original difficulties had by now been ironed out and the staff was able to focus on the main business of the School: to provide a unique learning experience.

There continued to be a severe shortage of money and there remained the need for very careful budgeting; the student bursaries – an important development enabling students to

© Richard Hubert Smith

Kurt Equiluz with members of the instrumental ensemble during a 1989 Bach course.

There was no reason for me to interfere. I was very impressed. The School was unique and I had never in my life come across anything quite like it. I thought it was wonderful that the students had the opportunity to study for a whole week with outstanding teachers and consequently to study so intensively. It was brilliant idea to allow observers to pay to sit in and listen to the masterclasses and I discovered such loyalty and enthusiasm among them. I always remember the way one would so often see David Heckels sitting at the back of the Recital Room listening to the classes. And there were many others who set aside the time to come to Snape and hear the young musicians and the teachers. Of course there was also the sheer magic of the place which so coloured the experience of the students and affected everybody who ever went to Snape.

SHEILA COLVIN
General Director, Aldeburgh Foundation

come to courses they could not otherwise afford, generously donated by individuals and organizations – still had to be carefully allocated.

John Owen had over the years devised schedules that were fair to everyone and that would produce the best results. He insisted that there were no alterations to these and students who tried to tamper with them soon learned to their cost that this was not a wise thing to do.

In earlier years there had often been two or three academic weekend courses, but from the late 1980s there was usually just one such course; the purely academic took a less central place in the schedule. There was, however, usually an academic element within each course with lectures given by experts – on the repertoire being studied or the composer. Students continued to enjoy invaluable access to the Britten–Pears Library and the Holst Library.

In April the regular French Song course took place with Hugues Cuénod and Suzanne Danco. Ian Bostridge was one of the students and Danco, who was always a very demanding teacher, was very severe with him. 'She gave him a really bad time,' one of the observers said and her sharp remarks are seared on to the memories of some of the students who were present at the time. However, by the end of the course, Suzanne Danco was commending him: 'He is the student who has taken the most notice of what I have been saying and the one who has learned the most.' The great British mezzo-soprano and Handel interpreter, Sarah Connolly, was also on this course.

After the Voice and Piano Duo course that followed, Heather Harper and Anthony Rolfe Johnson directed a course entitled 'Roles from the Britten Operas' and the Britten–Pears Orchestra, led by Gonzalo Acosta, gave a concert in the Festival conducted by Peter Maag and Richard Bernas with Hugh Maguire and Nobuko Imai performing the Mozart *Sinfonia concertante.*

Anthony Rolfe Johnson had been appointed Director of Singing Studies (a position Nancy Evans had held since the death of Peter Pears) at the start of this season and Heather Harper was for a period his co-Director. Harper's extensive singing career had taken in operatic roles ranging from Mozart to Wagner; she had been a notable Ellen Orford in *Peter Grimes* and Governess in *The Turn of the Screw*, and her concert appearances had included the first performance of *War Requiem.* Rolfe Johnson had a long and close association with the School and the Aldeburgh Festival. He was loved by students and staff alike and all who knew him were saddened by his debilitating illness and death at such a young age in 2010.

Following the decision taken by the Education Policy Committee the School did not present a fully-fledged opera in the 1989 Festival but, as a compromise, on 25 June, a semi-staged performance of Ravel's *L'Enfant et les sortilèges* and excerpts from Bizet's *Djamileh* were presented, with singers from the School and the Aldeburgh Chamber Choir; the Britten–Pears Orchestra was conducted by Steuart Bedford and led by Gonzalo Acosta. The pianists on the course were Nancy

Anthony Rolfe Johnson guiding Richard Edgar-Wilson during a 2000 course

Mozart: Don Giovanni
Britten–Mozart Festival, 1989

Don Giovanni	Richard Halton
	Charles Johnston
Commendatore	Nigel Fair
	Paul Sketris
Donna Anna	Anna Leanne Fjetland
	Patricia Hurd
Don Ottavio	Tony Boutté
	Mark Padmore
Donna Elvira	Cristen Gregory
	Rosalind Martin
Leporello	William Berges
	Desmond Byrne
Masetto	Graham Webber
Zerlina	Leslie Fagan
	Tinuke Olafimihan

Britten–Pears Orchestra
Conducted by Steuart Bedford
Course Director Suzanne Danco

Cooley, Jonathan Darlington and William Hancox. Among the students on this course was Michael Schade, the brilliantly successful Canadian tenor.

The rest of the year followed the familiar pattern. Max Rostal gave a series of masterclasses; the Thirteenth International Academy of String Quartets was directed by William Pleeth and Milan Kampa; Ileana Cotrubas returned for a Bel Canto course and Kurt Equiluz, a distinguished Bach singer and Evangelist who had worked frequently with Nikolas Harnoncourt and Gustav Leonhardt in the 1970s, directed a Bach course and was then joined by Ian Partridge for German Song.

In October the School performed a semi-staged production of *Don Giovanni* in the Britten–Mozart Festival. The course was directed by Suzanne Danco with Steuart Bedford conducting. There were, as usual, two casts.

This was the first course attended by Mark Padmore who had been a Choral Scholar at King's College, Cambridge; he went on to sing with Les Arts Florissants and The Sixteen before embarking on his solo career. Now the leading Evangelist of his generation, he returned to the Britten–Pears Young Artist Programme at Easter 2011 to give a series of masterclasses and performances of the *St John Passion*.

It is fascinating to consider the subsequent careers of the young musicians who studied at the School. All went through the same strict audition process and were presumably of more or less the same high standard; some went on to star-studded futures and others seem to have vanished without trace.

The School year ended in November with an academic weekend directed by Donald Mitchell on Britten's Church Parables.

The 1990 season started in April with a Voice and Piano Duo course. This was the first year that Caroline Dowdle was selected as one of the pianists. She became a regular pianist on courses at the School and now has a flourishing career as an accompanist and chamber music player.

Also in April 1990, there was a BPO course with Kyung-Wha Chung as soloist and Hugh Maguire conducting. At the end of the month Hugues Cuénod and Suzanne Danco with Jana Papandopulo returned to direct the French Song course. Sophie Daneman, who has been particularly successful in the baroque repertoire and who has sung with William Christie and Les Arts Florissants, was a student on this course, her first at Snape. At the end of April Jill Gomez and Ian Partridge directed a Britten Song course.

In the Festival of 1990 Anna Steiger again sang in a BPO concert, this time conducted by Lukas Foss. The orchestra was led by Katherine Loram and the timpanist for that concert was Simon Carrington, who was later principal timpanist with the London Symphony Orchestra. The School presented a semi-staged performance (thus not contravening the ban on fully staged opera by the School) of Purcell's *Dido and Aeneas* directed by John Shirley-Quirk, with the BPO conducted by Martin Isepp. Sophie Daneman sang the role of First Witch.

© Richard Hubert Smith

Tinuke Olafimihan (Zerlina) and Charles Johnston (Don Giovanni)

© Marco Borgrevve

Mark Padmore

*I was very keen to go to Aldeburgh after I saw the film [*The Aldeburgh Story, *Channel 4] made about the course on* Così fan tutte, *which was directed by Murray Perahia. I was very impressed by his playing of the tenor aria 'Un'aura amorosa', which was more musical and more intense than anything I had heard before and I was keen to study with people of that stature. I was inspired by the detailed work and the intensity of engagement that I saw in the film.*

I went to Snape and I just loved it; there was such special energy and everything was devoted to serious study. Steuart Bedford is one of the classiest and most knowledgeable of conductors and I got so much out of working with him. Suzanne Danco was a very fierce lady but she was right to be so and she had such feeling for the text. I found Nancy Evans so warm and encouraging and it was a privilege to work with people who had such close connections with Britten and Pears. I very much regret that I didn't get to Snape earlier – I would have loved to have worked with Peter Pears. The two opera courses that I did (1989 and 1990) really marked the beginning of my solo career.

MARK PADMORE

The String Courses in 1990 followed the established pattern. Max Rostal returned for a Solo Violin course, and a Chamber Music course, with six participating piano trios, was directed by George Malcolm, Hugh Maguire and William Pleeth.

The String Quartet course, which by this point had an unbroken fourteen-year history, was directed by Thomas Kakuska, Günther Pichler and Hugh Maguire. In July and August Ruggiero Ricci returned to give a series of Solo Violin masterclasses.

In August Vishnevskaya held the Russian Song masterclasses and Ileana Cotrubas a Mozart Song course, and in September a German Oratorio course took place with Kurt Equiluz. This was followed by Roles from the Britten Operas with Anthony Rolfe Johnson, Heather Harper and Theodor Uppman.

A study course on Britten's opera *Billy Budd* with Theodor Uppman, who had created the title role, ran in parallel with the Britten Roles course.

In October the School embarked on a Britten–Verdi opera course, which included a semi-staged performance of *Falstaff* in the Maltings. The opera was directed by the great Italian baritone Renato Cappecchi and in many ways returned to the original concept of presenting School operas with simple but effective staging, using the distinctive Maltings screens and minimal props. The Britten–Pears Orchestra was conducted by Steuart Bedford.

Mark Padmore, who sang the role of Fenton, remarked on Cappecchi's direction from which, he said, he gained many

© *Richard Hubert Smith*

The not-so-merry gentlemen of Windsor in Verdi's *Falstaff*. Mark Padmore (Fenton) is second from the right.

© Arno Drucker

Kathy Wolfenden with Elly Ameling

valuable insights. Mary Plazas sang Nanetta; she had previously attended the Voice and Piano Duos course with Janine Reiss. Plazas has since had a successful international career and for a number of years was a company principal at ENO where she was Anthony Minghella's first Cio-Cio San in his much admired production of *Madam Butterfly*. Plazas continued her association with Aldeburgh by appearing as the Duchess in Thomas Adès's *Powder Her Face* at the Festival – a role that she also recorded for a Channel 4 film of the opera.

In 1991 John Owen left the School to start his own business as an artists' agent and manager. His influence had been crucial throughout the development of the School. Kathy Wolfenden was appointed as his successor.

The courses in 1991 followed the familiar pattern with almost no changes to what had become the yearly routine of international auditions to select students showing marked potential for a familiar sequence of courses led by teachers who returned so frequently to Snape that they had virtually become permanent members of staff.

Although there was an understanding by the Directors and the staff that a successful pattern was in place, any resting on laurels was firmly resisted and the aim for constant improvement remained to the fore, building on the core values of the School's founders.

One has only to hear the tributes paid by former students and to follow their subsequent careers to be made aware of the profound effect that the School has had on the musical profession. Benjamin Britten, Peter Pears and Imogen Holst, who had first dreamed of establishing a centre for musical education in Suffolk, had all died during the course of the dream becoming a reality. Pears had lived to see the School at its most influential and effective. After the nineteen years that had passed since the first masterclasses were held in the Maltings everybody who taught, studied or worked at the School knew what an enormous debt of gratitude was owed to the three of them. And so many students felt that the links to these founders were still vibrant and that this was the place where their influence could still be felt.

It has been the goal of this short history to chart the way in which the School grew and developed and how it overcame the practical difficulties inherent in such an endeavour. None of it could have been achieved without the support, financial and practical, given by the Britten–Pears Foundation, which was determined to see the original vision become a reality. There were others, too, without whose contribution this success could not have been realized: the many donors and sponsors who helped to raise the essential funding; the teachers, coaches and accompanists who often accepted fees much lower than they would normally command and who were prepared to give of their very best to the students, and the staff who worked extraordinarily long hours uncomplainingly for comparatively low salaries.

When they look back on their days at Snape, it is startling how often former students, teachers and accompanists use the words 'magic' or 'magical'. There was, indeed, something magical about the environment in which they all worked, something that is replicated nowhere else.

Success came as the result of a spirit of dedication and devotion to its founders' vision that characterized the School in its first years. No effort was considered too great to ensure that it succeeded. All over the world those who benefited from this unique place remember it with affection and respect.

This is far from being the end of the story. Over the last two decades the School has adapted to meet the changing needs of the musical world it serves. Those developments are the concern of the final section of this book.

The Present and the Future

Until 1997 the umbrella organization for the School, the Festival and the Snape Maltings Concert Hall was the Aldeburgh Foundation. In 1998 it became Aldeburgh Productions and in 2007 was rebranded as Aldeburgh Music. Since 2003, the original concept of Benjamin Britten and Peter Pears, guiding young musicians in the early stages of their professional careers, has been the responsibility of the Britten–Pears Young Artist Programme, which has become known familiarly as the 'BPP'. This change of name encapsulates the developing ethos of the educational work undertaken at Snape.

When Jonathan Reekie was appointed as Chief Executive in 1997, he inherited a management structure for the School and a calendar of courses from his predecessor Sheila Colvin, the General Manager of Aldeburgh Productions, and Kathy Wolfenden, the School's Administrator. This was largely unchanged from the days of Kenneth Baird and John Owen.

He had to deal with yet another financial crisis requiring urgent attention as it threatened to engulf the entire organization and to consider the fundamental and dramatic changes in the world of music education throughout Europe. What the School was offering was no longer unique.

The period when great international artists agreed to come to teach at Snape, simply because Peter Pears or his musical colleagues and friends invited them, was now at an end. There was certainly a sense of continuity: artists such as Elly Ameling and Joan Sutherland, who had experience of working with Britten and/or Pears earlier in their careers, came to teach at the School for the first time long after both founders had died, and a new generation of teachers – including Mark Padmore and Roger Vignoles – who had first become familiar with the School and its ethos as students or accompanists, returned to take responsibility for courses. However, eleven years after the death of Peter Pears, the cosy family attitudes of the early days had evaporated and the atmosphere had changed irrevocably.

The School administrators were no longer finding it easy to attract the finest international teachers or students of the highest musical quality from across the world. The vision underpinning the work of the Britten–Pears School might have been influenced originally by the programmes at Tanglewood and Banff but what it had offered students in Britain at its inception was unique. Its founders and everyone involved in its early development had given it an unassailable status within the UK. However, over time, that influence had waned and the model of the School had been widely copied. There were now innumerable opportunities for students to study intensively with outstanding teachers.

Music education was very much in vogue with fund-giving bodies of all kinds, and programmes for young artists were being set up by a great variety of musical organizations, including opera houses and orchestras. The environment at Snape continued to be considered ideal for serious study but travelling to Suffolk requires a degree of effort and many students were tempted by these newly established programmes to remain in the cities.

Jonathan Reekie was determined to re-establish the School's reputation as an educational centre of the very highest standard. He recognized that change was inevitable. The original concept had been perfect for the 1970s and the 1980s but was no longer viable in the contemporary financial and educational ambience. While acknowledging that it was essential to take account of the way the world around the School had changed, Reekie also believed that if Snape were once again to become the foremost place to study music in Britain, it was essential to rediscover and re-interpret the principles that had been fundamental to the concept of the School.

When Reekie took over the management of the organization, he was surprised to find a marked lack of integration and cohesion between the different components. The Festival and the School might once have operated very closely together but Reekie found that by the late 1990s they had become two virtually entirely separate bodies. What had once been perceived as a danger was now established as the status quo. Further, Reekie was concerned to find that there was a temptation for the Festival to exploit the School's students to minimize its own costs.

In his initial assessment, Reekie recognized that the vocal courses continued to offer tuition of outstanding quality. Although Peter Pears and his immediate friends and colleagues were no longer there to bring their own personal friends and musical collaborators to the School, the list of teachers who had brought their skills and experience to the School since 1991 was as distinguished as it had ever been. It included Thomas Allen, Elly Ameling, Michael Chance, Anne Evans, Sergey Leiferkus, Ann Murray, Joan Rodgers and Joan Sutherland. The composition courses too were flourishing, bringing creative young composers to Snape and offering them opportunities and guidance unimaginable elsewhere (see pp. 213–15).

Where Reekie identified a major problem was in the instrumental side of the curriculum. The School seemed no longer to be able to attract the highest quality of students. This was clearly reflected in the work of the Britten–Pears Orchestra, which Reekie felt was not being managed efficiently to realize its full potential. 'Putting this right has been an enormous challenge,' he said in late 2011. 'I hope that by next year we shall have crossed the threshold.'

Meeting these challenges led to what seemed to many the radical step of changing the name to the Britten–Pears Young Artist Programme. 'It was designed to signal to the world that we were moving on,' says Reekie, 'that we needed again to become more international and unlock the potential of what Aldeburgh could be and had once been. It just seemed to be the right thing to do and now it is starting to bear fruit.'

There have been other innovations: among them, the very successful Aldeburgh Residency Programme. For many years there had been residencies tailored for string quartets. Reekie saw the possibility of extending this idea to embrace ensembles of slightly more experienced musicians with perhaps more established careers and offer them the opportunity to come to Aldeburgh and Snape to concentrate intensively on an area of their choice. Since 2004, the Residency Programme has allowed musicians to enjoy the sense of freedom that Snape provides, to take advantage of the facilities and the opportunity to hone their skills. Snape offers these performers, often at a juncture in their careers where they are exploring new ways of presenting their work or exploring new repertoire, an environment where their creative development can be fully supported. This formula has proved very successful: in 2011, for example, Mitsuko Uchida directed residency masterclasses with an ensemble that included BPP alumni from the 2007 Beethoven course that had been led by members of the Florestan Trio. Uchida was able to work intensively with the participants and the classes were open to the general public.

In recent years residencies have included the vocal ensemble I Fagiolini developing its *Tallis in Wonderland* programme, which was premiered at the 2009 Aldeburgh Easter Festival; also in 2009 theatre director Tom Morris working with the Sacconi Quartet on a theatrical interpretation of Beethoven's Op. 131 String Quartet; pianists Paul Lewis and Steven Osborne preparing Schubert works for four hands in 2010, as well as the continuation of the long-established spring season of young string quartets extending their repertoire and giving popular public lunchtime concerts in the Jubilee Hall.

Although Jonathan Reekie's appointment was the catalyst for much of the development of the BPP, there were also initiatives dating from an earlier period that had proved

Jonathan Reekie

As a trio we were so excited to travel to Aldeburgh to meet and work with Mitsuko Uchida, someone that we had huge respect for. Not only were our lessons extremely productive, the opportunities to socialize with her were most inspiring. She is full of fascinating anecdotes and loves to talk about music. The passion that she conveys can't help but be transferred to everyone around her. The course concluded with a concert of Schubert trios and Schoenberg's Pierrot lunaire. *For us, the latter particularly caught our imaginations! Overall, it was an all-round fantastic experience.*

MEMBER OF THE RHODES TRIO

valuable and which still form an important part of the programme.

The Contemporary Performance and Composition courses were first scheduled in 1992 and were led by Oliver Knussen, Colin Matthews and Magnus Lindberg. One of the first students on this course was Thomas Adès, who subsequently became Artistic Director of the Aldeburgh Festival. The course now runs in alternate years with Contemporary Alumni concerts in the Festival showcasing the compositions created during the course. This course has become a very important feature of the BPP; in 2011 Francisco Coll, who had attended the 2009 course, had his Aldeburgh Festival premiere and subsequently agreed a contract with Faber Music.

A further innovation for young composers is the New Music New Media course which concentrates on new technology and different media and allows students to work with some of the foremost innovators in their field.

Aldeburgh Young Musicians is a project that dates from 2008. Its aim is to support talented young performers aged between eight and eighteen in the belief that they might one day benefit from study at the BPP. In the current season, 2011–12, forty-three young musicians have participated in masterclasses, tutorials and concerts during the school holidays, working with world-class musicians and teachers.

The Britten–Pears Baroque Orchestra, formed to explore the baroque repertoire and to support the growing number of musicians who choose to explore this path, both vocally and

Continued on page 216

Oliver Knussen, who was invited to become an Artistic Director of the Festival by Peter Pears in 1983, and I had long thought of the possibility of setting up an Aldeburgh equivalent to the composing course run by the Boston Symphony Orchestra at Tanglewood since the 1940s. (Tanglewood had seen the USA premiere of Peter Grimes *in 1946.)*

In 1991 I began an association with the London Symphony Orchestra, and for a time it seemed as if an LSO summer residency at Snape might incorporate a composition element; but this fell through, largely because of the impracticality of finding adequate accommodation for an orchestra.

Olly and I nevertheless went ahead with plans for a composition course, incorporating a performance element on a much smaller scale, and six young composers (among them Thomas Adès and Julian Anderson) took part in the first course at the Britten–Pears School in July 1992.

The model set up then has been followed ever since, usually in alternate years : the composers are asked to write a work in less than a week; this is then rehearsed and performed by an ensemble of around fifteen players, who during the ten days of the course work intensively at a wide range of contemporary repertoire under the direction of distinguished instrumentalists. Singers have also taken part in the course from time to time, and Magnus Lindberg has been the guest composition director in most years since 1994. More recently the course has been featured as one of the 'alumni' concerts held during the

© Maurice Foxall

Colin Matthews

Festival, offering the composers an opportunity to rework and refine their original compositions, and a public platform. Between 1992 and 2011 no fewer than sixty-seven composers have taken part.

COLIN MATTHEWS

1992

Thomas Adès Julian Anderson Paul Newland
Russell Platt Alwynne Pritchard Yong Yan

1994

Thomas Armstrong Richard Causton David Knotts
Joseph Phibbs Huw Watkins

1995

John Cooney Sam Hayden Edward Rushton Paul Whitty

1997

David Bruce Francisco Lara Stuart Macrae
Ketty Nez Doug Opel

1998

Jonathan Cole Maud Hodson Stuart Macrae
Russell Millard Kurt Rohde

2000

Luke Bedford Ben Foskett John B. Hedges Mark Horton
David Ludwig Arlene Sierra Stefan Wirth

2001

Matthew Brooks   Tom Evans   Phillip Martin
James Olsen   Oliver Searle

2003

Richard Fitzhugh   Emily Hall   Jordan Hunt
Anna Meredith   Matthew Rogers

2005

Daniel Basford   Elspeth Brooke   Helen Grime
Tom Littlewood   Geoff Paterson   Matthew Rogers

2007

Charlotte Bray   Steven Daverson   Vlad Maistorovici
Chris Mayo   Sean Shepherd   Sasha Siem

2009

Francisco Coll   Chris Gendall   Nancie Gynn
Joanna Lee   Edward Nesbit   Lauri Supponen

2011

Edmund Finnis   Arne Gieshoff   Matthew Kaner   Eric Nathan
Elizabeth Ogonek   Gilad Rabinovich   Elizabeth Winters

Oliver Knussen

© Nigel Luckhurst

Oliver Knussen with Jordan Hunt during rehearsals for a performance at Snape Maltings Concert Hall of Hunt's *Night Burst* in October 2004

instrumentally, was established in the early 1990s, with Ton Koopman directing the inaugural course. The ensemble has worked with the Orchestra of the Age of Enlightenment and the Freiburg Baroque Orchestra and now features regularly in Aldeburgh Music's annual programme.

This is a indication of the considerable change in emphasis from an occasion I remember in the early 1980s when Peter Pears held a press conference to announce the Festival programme and he came to an event featuring an ensemble playing authentic instruments. He smiled and said, 'But not too authentic, I hope.'

One of the most exciting and important projects ever to be conceived for the BPP is the Aldeburgh World Orchestra, which in 2012 will celebrate the fortieth anniversary of the first weekend of masterclasses at the Britten–Pears School. The year 2012 also sees the Cultural Olympiad, a recognition of the extraordinary growth in interest in the arts and classical music throughout the world. Classical music once seemed to be the province of Europe and North America but that is certainly no longer exclusively the case.

The extraordinary number of gifted young people in China studying and giving their whole lives to classical music demonstrates how important classical music has become in China and other Asian countries. El Sistema in Venezuela has changed the lives of innumerable children and brought joy in the performance of classical music into corners of society where it was previously entirely unknown. Young people in

Soweto have been introduced to classical music and discovered not only their own gifts and talents but a career path that has transformed their lives. All these factors led to the vision of the Aldeburgh World Orchestra.

This three-year project reaches its climax in 2012 as young musicians from every continent come together to form an orchestra to be conducted by Sir Mark Elder, giving performances as part of the Cultural Olympiad, the BBC Proms and at Snape Maltings Concert Hall following a residency with world-famous orchestral tutors – many of them BPP alumni – at Snape. One can hardly imagine a more fitting tribute to Britten and Pears than this imaginative, creative and far-reaching project.

The School has always been well served by its administrators. John Owen steered it safely through its difficult early years. He was followed by Kathy Wolfenden and she in turn was succeeded by Elizabeth Webb. During their time at the School they each pursued the tried and tested sequence of courses.

With the advent of Jonathan Reekie came the perception that without change the School would risk stagnation and certainly lose its position at the forefront of musical education in this country. He was well supported by Tisi Dutton during her time as Administrator and together they were able to begin to bring in the new initiatives that both thought were essential, and manage this challenging period of change and development as the Britten–Pears School made its transition into the Britten–Pears Young Artist Programme.

Tisi Dutton was followed in 2000 by Andrew Comben, who is currently the Chief Executive of the Brighton Festival. He recalls his period at Snape with enormous affection: 'It was a vital time for me,' he says. 'I felt I arrived at a moment of great importance in the development of the Britten–Pears Programme.' Comben agreed with Jonathan Reekie about the need to adapt to a changing world and he remembers long conversations between Reekie, Colin Matthews and himself about the future development of the BPP, with each of the three anxious to see the BPP restored to the cutting edge of musical education in Britain, once more attracting the most gifted students: 'We wanted the glorious times again but we knew that we couldn't just rely on the past and that a new vision was needed.'

Comben, too, was dismayed to find a lack of integration between the Festival, the Concert Hall and the School. He was astonished to discover that there was no shared history and, in fact, very little record of the past activities of the School. 'There were a few documents and papers in a cupboard upstairs, but very little else. If I wanted to find out who had attended a previous course or sung in an opera staged by the School, there appeared to be no way of doing so. It was incredibly difficult; records did exist but were certainly not readily available.'

Highlights recalled by Comben include a course in 2002 directed by Ann Murray. Murray's immediate rapport with student Lucy Crowe, her sympathy and understanding of the difficulties encountered by the young singer, have led to a lifelong friendship between the two women. He also recalls the production of *Ariadne auf Naxos* with Colin Graham making a last-minute return to the UK to direct it – the first time he had directed in the UK since his departure to the United States: 'What a triumph this was. Everybody on the course absolutely adored Colin and he got the very best out of all the singers. The work that he did with them will remain with them for ever.'

Comben was followed as Head of the BPP by first Anita Crowe and now Bill Lloyd, who points to the impact the £6m development of the new Hoffmann Building at Snape is having on the Young Artist Programme and Aldeburgh Residencies. The new studio theatre/concert hall is proving a perfect complement to the Maltings for smaller-scale and more intimate works.

Lloyd is enthusiastic about the growing integration of education and performance in the future plans of Aldeburgh Music. In 2011 the BPP provided a full day of events in the Aldeburgh Festival and the Festival's Artistic Director, Pierre Laurent Aimard, who performed alongside BPP students in 2011, will return to teach in 2012, when the faculty will also include Dawn Upshaw and Menahem Pressler, who will give masterclasses as well as perform at the Festival. Lloyd considers it vital that young artists get the opportunity to hear their mentors in performance. He also plans to increase the time performers and composers spend together, with composers joining string quartet and vocal courses to try out their ideas and hone their skills with the performers who are likely to be presenting their work – one hopes – for many years to come.

Apart from these changes and innovations the lives of the students attending courses at Snape continue in much the same way. However, there are now excellent catering facilities and cheese or ham buns are no longer the only form of sustenance on offer. The character of Aldeburgh itself has altered and in recent years it has become a much more fashionable place, with bed-and-breakfast establishments growing more sophisticated and catering for the visitors who, unlike the students in the early days, demand high standards – including constant hot water. Aldeburgh Music was able to purchase a large building in the High Street to provide hostel accommodation for the students. Communal living for the students has taken the place of the surrogate family life offered by their landladies.

My conversation with Jonathan Reekie gave me a sense of the very long journey that began with the first masterclass weekend in 1972: a weekend that now seems to have been more of a private, family affair than the beginning of a musical establishment respected and recognized throughout the world. One can recall the endless doubts and disagreements over the future structure of the School and the aim, which was at one time shared by Dr Swinburne and others, to see it develop into a full-time educational institution funded by central government.

Mercifully the School was given the freedom to evolve in its own distinctive manner with everybody involved feeling for a way ahead and learning from mistakes. It is clear that allowing the School to grow in this way – although it might have tried the patience of some involved in the early stages – was the best path to follow and the closest to the original vision of its founders. Without their dedication and the dedication of countless benefactors, teachers, students and administrative staff, none of this would have happened. In 2012, forty years after the first masterclasses, all can take pride and satisfaction in the achievements of what is now the Britten–Pears Young Artist Programme.

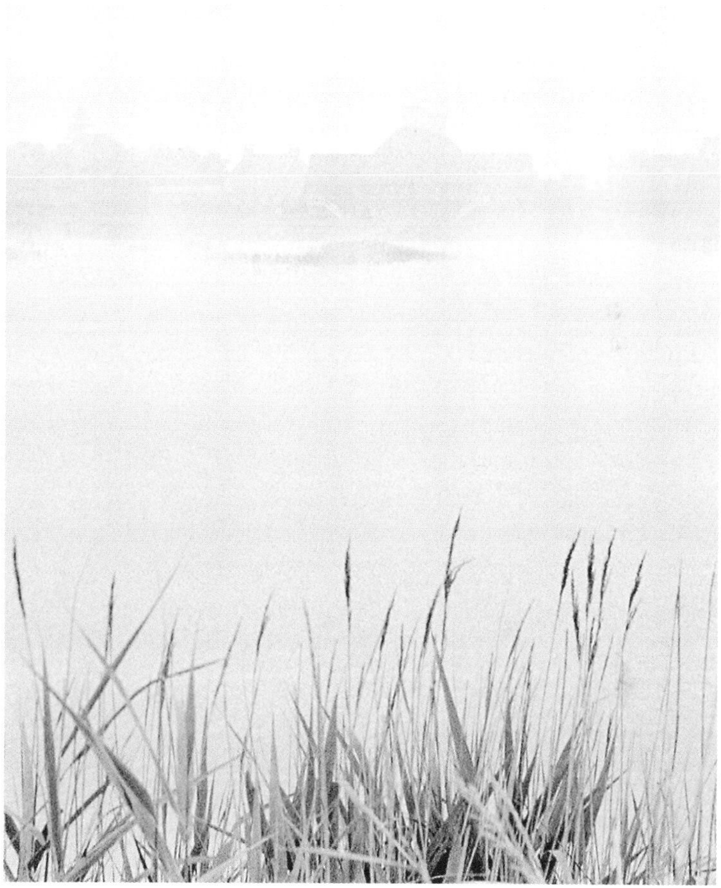

© Nigel Luckhurst

'The Maltings has a very special atmosphere – the light on the marshes and the intimacy of the surroundings lending it a spiritual aura that seeps into you after a few days and never really leaves you.' – Jonathan Darlington

PART-TITLE IMAGES

p. 12 View of the River Alde from the Maltings
© Nigel Luckhurst

p. 20 The Maltings and the grain store building that was to be converted into the Britten–Pears School
© Nigel Luckhurst

p. 90 The bronze busts of Benjamin Britten and Peter Pears by Georg Ehrlich displayed in the Entrance Hall of the Britten–Pears School
© Nigel Luckhurst

p. 192 The students acknowledge the audience at the conclusion of an end-of-course concert in the Recital Room at the Britten–Pears School. Phyllis Bryn-Julson, the director of the English and American Song course, stands centre, with vocal coach Ruth Drucker to the left of her.
© Arno Drucker

p. 208 The Maltings Concert Hall with the School building far left. Far right is Barbara Hepworth's sculpture, three figures from the nine-part *The Family of Man* (1970).
© Nigel Luckhurst

ACKNOWLEDGEMENT OF COPYRIGHT TEXTS

The text of the interval talk given by Imogen Holst is reproduced by kind permission of The Holst Foundation.

While every reasonable effort has been made to identify copyright holders of text or images reproduced in this book, the author and publishers apologize for any inadvertent omissions and would be pleased to hear from any unacknowledged copyright-holders.

Index

References to images are shown in *italic* type and to displayed quotations in **bold** type.